I0530418

ANGER MANAGEMENT FOR EXPLOSIVE PARENTS

SUPER STRATEGIES FOR MOMS AND DADS TO CALM YOUR TEMPER, UNDERSTAND YOUR TRIGGERS AND CONTROL YOUR EMOTIONS

REMINGTON JAMES

TABLE OF CONTENTS

INTRODUCTION

When I was seven years old, I gave myself a haircut.

I didn't mean to. My mom had left her hair scissors on the dining-room table, and I wanted to cut something. So, first, I cut some paper from the math copybook. Then, I cut the dress of my little sister's doll. Then I cut some of my hair. I liked the sound the scissors made as they sliced through my hair. So, I did it again. And again. Then, a few more times before I got bored.

When my dad got home, he walked into the living room, where I was sitting on the sofa, playing a video game. He looked at me, and his face immediately got red.

"What the hell did you do?" he shouted.

I looked up, startled and confused. "Nothing," I said.

"What happened to your head?"

"Nothing," I said.

"Why the hell did you cut your hair?" he yelled.

By then, I couldn't even speak. All I remember afterward was him pulling me up violently by my arm and bundling me into the car, all the while muttering under his breath about dumb children. Then he drove me to the barber to fix the damage I had done.

The barber himself was amused. "Do you want to take away my job, young man?"

My father was still fuming, though. And my arm ached for days after.

* * *

Jump ahead thirty years, and I'm at a funeral for the father of Shane, one of my best friends since high school. Shane's father was just sixty-seven when he died. This was a man who should have lived to his 80s. He ran a marathon every year, didn't smoke, drank only socially, and ate sensibly. But, with no warning, he got prostate cancer, which progressed so quickly that he was dead a year later. Shane told me that his father remained his usual cheerful self all through the chemo and never acted as though life had been unfair. Yet, Shane himself was angry that his father died before he should have due to a disease that should have been curable.

In his eulogy, Shane told a story about his first day at high school. He took the bus home, and when he walked into the house, his father was in the living room and asked two questions: "How was your day? Where's your school bag?"

Shane had left it on the bus. So, he and his dad jumped into the car and sped off, looking for the bus, which they caught up to ten minutes later.

"He wasn't even bothered," Shane told the mourners. "He just laughed at me and set about fixing the problem."

* * *

I tell these two stories to show how your actions as a parent stick with your children. Decades later, I still remember how my father was mad at me that day. Not all my memories of him are negative, but that one is always there in my head when I think about him. For Shane, on the other hand, his main memory is about his dad not getting angry about something but instead making it into a small father-son adventure.

If you're reading this book, you're most likely worried about how your anger issues are affecting your child or children. You're probably worried about how it will affect their love for you. You might be even more worried about how your anger might mess them up as adults.

You're right to be concerned about the first, but you shouldn't worry too much about the second. In this book, I'll show you the research that proves your anger doesn't drastically affect your child's life outcomes. However, your anger will probably affect the kind of relationship you have with them as teenagers and as adults.

If that relationship is broken, it gets harder to repair the older your kids are. It's not impossible, just harder. If your children are still small, then now is the time to get control of your anger issues. That is the main goal of this book—to offer proven techniques for identifying your triggers, controlling or directing your rage, and, most importantly, repairing your relationship with your children of any age.

In Chapter One, we look at the main cause of anger—the stresses of parenting. As you already know, life after children is completely different from life before. You're really a different person now, and you need to learn new ways to understand and manage your new self.

In Chapter Two, we provide a practical toolkit based on leading research to manage anger (the C.A.L.M.S. Anger Management Toolkit). Chapter Three shows you how to identify the triggers that set off your rage. Once you understand these, you almost automatically get better at controlling or directing your anger. In case you're wondering, I include "directing" because anger is sometimes a productive response, even with your children. In Chapter Four, which is titled "Always Stay Calm," we examine this in detail.

Chapter Five looks at communicating effectively with your children, especially when they're making you angry. Chapter Six deals with keeping a positive mindset while acknowledging your anger. In Chapter Seven, we examine support systems. This is important because, more than any one of the six basic emotions, anger is the one that makes us believe we're always right. (The other five emotions are sadness, happiness, fear, surprise, and disgust.) Thus, we need help from other people to deal with our anger objectively.

In Chapter Eight, we look at ways to track your progress. Chapter Nine, which ends the book, provides practical strategies for anger management that you can use every day as a parent.

Once you apply the information in this book, you will almost immediately see an improvement in your relationship with your kid or kids. That alone will make your life better. You'll also worry less about them. Just as importantly, you will come to a better understanding of yourself. As Socrates said, "The unexamined life is not worth living."

Turn the page to pass your examination on being a better parent and a better person.

1

UNDERSTANDING PARENTAL STRESS AND ITS IMPACTS

One of the most dangerous features of anger is that anger calls forth anger, and the cycle can rapidly escalate.[1]

— PAUL EKMAN, PSYCHOLOGIST

This chapter looks at how parental stress fuels anger and how that affects the family. We'll look at the most common stressors: balancing work and family life, managing children's behavioral issues, and finances. But first, let's examine the wolverine in the room: anger itself.

Out of all the emotions, anger is viewed most negatively by most people. We do not like it when anger is directed at us, and we often do not like it when we become angry. Yet anger, like all emotions, helps us to function effectively as human beings.

---

1. Paul Ekman, *Emotions Revealed*, Hachette, 2004, p. 112.

Psychologist Paul Ekman, one of the world's leading experts on emotional expression, says, "Even anger—the emotion most people would like to turn off—is useful to us. It warns others, and us as well, when things are thwarting us . . . Anger tells us that something needs to change. If we are to bring about that change most effectively, we need to know the source of our anger."[2]

Anger exists across a spectrum, from annoyance to rage. It underlies a range of experiences: indignation, sulking, exasperation, resentment, hatred, and revenge. Unfortunately, we are more likely to get angry (in all these forms) with the people we are close to. As Ekman points out, there is no paradox here.

"Disappointment in how a person has acted may also make us angry, especially when that person is someone we care deeply about," he writes. "It may seem strange that we can get the angriest at those we love the most, but those are the people who can hurt and disappoint us the most."[3]

This is why parents are more likely to get angry with their children, who they love more than anything else in the world (except burgers, the New York Yankees, and sleep).

So, as you read this book, bear in mind that your goal is not to stop feeling anger (a probably impossible task in any case). It is to control, direct, and, sometimes, suppress it.

That said, let's look at how parenting itself makes us more prone to anger.

2. Ekman, *Emotions Revealed*, pp. 43, 125.
3. Ekman, *Emotions Revealed*, p. 112.

TAKE THIS PARENTING AND SHOVE IT!

Mike Fisher, who founded the British Association of Anger Management in 1999, has extensive experience dealing with the effects of anger on both children and parents. Over two decades, he has worked with tens of thousands of individuals, helping them manage and understand their anger. Fisher notes that around 20% of his clients are middle-class, well-educated, and affluent parents, indicating that anger issues cut across socioeconomic lines and often involve social services.[4]

Fisher points out that parental pressure often stems from their upbringing. Some parents strive not to repeat their parents' mistakes, overcompensating in the process, while others try to emulate their excellent parenting, leading to competitive stress. As children grow, parents may find themselves better suited to different stages of their children's development, which can create imbalances and affect family dynamics. For instance, some parents might handle infancy better, while others are more adept at managing the teenage years. This disparity can strain the family system and lead to increased stress and conflict.

Fisher emphasizes the importance of not demonizing parents who express anger, recognizing that such anger often comes from a place of deep care and sensitivity. He notes that people who get angry about their children's behavior often care deeply and are highly sensitive to their children's needs. However, despite their good intentions, these parents may still struggle to manage their emotions effectively, which can negatively impact their children.

4. Nicola Skinner, "Why Parents Are Getting Angrier: 'Children Are Bored out of Their Skulls with Real Life,'" *The Guardian*, September 3, 2016, sec. Life and style, https://www.theguardian.com/lifeandstyle/2016/sep/03/why-parents-are-getting-angrier-children-are-bored-out-of-their-skulls-with-real-life.

Psychologists define parenting stress as the distress experienced when the demands of parenting exceed your capacity to handle them.[5] This happens when you feel overwhelmed and believe you lack the resources to be a good parent.

What causes parenting stress? To a certain extent, it's rooted in your state of mind. Stress, after all, is internal, i.e., it's rooted in our response to external events. The same event—a three-year-old refusing to get into the car to go to preschool, for example—will send one parent into a rage while another will go into cajole mode, while a third will tell the child he's turned into a sack of potatoes and pick him up and fling him playfully into the backseat.

A person who believes they have the competence to be a good parent is less likely to be stressed than one who believes they suck at this parenting job (which is pretty much all of us when we first have a child). Research shows a strong link between parental self-efficacy, parenting stress, and overall well-being. Parents who believe in their parenting capabilities tend to report lower levels of stress and better mental health.

This connection makes sense because feeling inadequate, being overwhelmed, and struggling to meet parental responsibilities—all markers of low self-efficacy—are the same indicators psychologists use to identify parenting stress. What makes it worse is that parents with low self-efficacy are more likely to have children with difficult temperaments. This is, for the most part, genetic (I'll get more into this later in this chapter) and partly a vicious cycle (the parents' stress stresses the child, whose behavior then becomes harder to control). The objective circumstances also exacerbate the situation: stressed parents have lower levels of social support,

---

5. Gwen Dewar, "Parenting Stress: What Causes It, and How Does It Change Us?" PARENTING SCIENCE, March 1, 2024, https://parentingscience.com/parent ing-stress/

making them more likely to fly off the handle, which further reduces their confidence in their parenting abilities.

The silver lining here is that improving your self-efficacy can significantly reduce stress levels. Various effective stress management techniques can help parents cope with daily challenges and retrain their thought patterns to experience real relief, which we'll get into in the next chapter. However, it is essential to acknowledge that not all parenting stress originates from the parent's mindset, nor do all parents face the same challenges.

5 MAIN CAUSES OF PARENTAL STRESS

If you're a stressed parent of young children, don't worry; there's light at the end of the tunnel. The only problem is it will take between twenty to twenty-five years to get there. The research shows that parents tend to become less stressed when their children are grown and independent. (That's assuming they don't grow up to be drug addicts, exotic dancers, or members of Congress.) Additionally, parents report greater well-being if they have strong social support and children without significant issues, such as those with easy temperaments and good physical and emotional health.

However, certain situations are almost guaranteed to make parenting more stressful and thus bring out your angry side. These are:

1. A child with a difficult temperament
2. A child with medical, emotional, or behavioral problems
3. Low levels of support
4. Being a single parent
5. Having a young child

These factors can diminish parental well-being, as they mean a heavier burden. Some challenges are particularly tough, such as coping with a child's externalizing problems like aggression and defiance. Studies suggest that managing these behaviors is more stressful than dealing with internalizing issues such as depression or anxiety. Stress levels are typically high for parents raising children on the autism spectrum or other developmental disorders, especially if the parents don't have enough social support or financial resources.

Interestingly, the item "having a young child" warrants further discussion. Research suggests that the youngest children, especially babies, are often associated with the lowest levels of parenting stress. However, many parents find their stress levels increase significantly when their children reach middle school.

Determining the most stressful age for parenting likely varies based on cultural factors and individual family dynamics. Nonetheless, two large studies conducted in the United States offer valuable insights. In both studies, researchers surveyed thousands of parents and found that stress levels were relatively low when children were infants. As children grew older, stress levels increased, peaking during the preschool and middle school years in one study. Another study noted a consistent trend of elevated stress for parents of children between six and seventeen years old.

American mothers working outside the home experience the greatest job pressure and financial strain when their children are infants. The upside is that parents often find greater psychological rewards during their children's early years, even though these years can be more physically exhausting. During infancy and preschool years, parents receive more love and less defiance from their children. And then they become teenagers.

Social factors—which might perhaps be more precisely called political policies—also affect parental stress. Compared to childless individuals, parents fare worse in countries where they receive fewer subsidies and lack family-friendly work policies. The United States ranks the worst in this regard, with Ireland, the United Kingdom, and New Zealand close behind.[6] Who knew that how you voted would affect whether you yell at your 12-year-old for flinging their jacket on the floor instead of in the laundry hamper?

Other causes of stress include:

- Anxiety related to work
- Financial difficulties
- Struggles with work-life balance
- Family planning issues
- Managing a household
- Parent burnout
- Conflicts with other caregivers (such as ex-spouses, daycare providers, or teachers)
- Caring for elderly parents
- Lack of social support

According to the 2023 American Family Survey, the most significant challenge facing American families is the financial burden associated with raising children. This issue overshadows other significant concerns, including the impact of technology—such as social media and video games—which is tied to "high work

---

6. Jennifer Glass, Robin W. Simon, and Matthew A. Andersson, "Parenthood and Happiness: Effects of Work-Family Reconciliation Policies in 22 OECD Countries," *American Journal of Sociology* 122, no. 3 (November 2016): 886–929, https://doi.org/10.1086/688892.

demands and parental stress" for the second most significant challenge.[7]

American parents worry about affording family life and meeting the demands of inflation. The survey also identified other major concerns impacting families, such as children growing up in single-parent homes and dealing with mental and physical health issues. These challenges round out the top five, surpassing other concerns like family violence, lack of educational opportunities, sexual permissiveness, substance abuse, and crime. These latter issues were each mentioned by no more than 12.5% of respondents, indicating they are perceived as less pressing compared to financial and health-related concerns.

Interestingly, Americans tend to have a positive view of their own family situations: more than 75% of adults report being satisfied with their families, while only 11% express dissatisfaction. This positive outlook on personal family life contrasts with the broader concerns they have about the family unit as a social institution.

A STRESSED PARENT IS NO PARENT

Stress can significantly impair our ability to be attentive and sensitive to our children's needs, thoughts, and emotions. This diminished sensitivity can manifest in both our brain function and our behaviors. Stressed parents often overreact to their children's actions, losing their temper quickly or becoming upset too easily. Sometimes, stress has the opposite effect: Parents become

---

7. Christopher F. Karpowitz and Jeremy C. Pope, "2023 REPORT The Practicalities and Politicization of American Family Life," The American Family Survey. Center for the Study of Elections and Democracy &The Wheatley Institute, 2023, https://media.deseret.com/media/misc/pdf/afs/2023-american-family-survey. pdf?_gl=1*2d9gns*_ga*MTYwNjc2Njc4NC4xNzIxNDIxNDUx*_ga_YNR-PD2MVFD*MTcyMTQyMTQ1MS4xLjEuMTcyMTQyMjk5Ni41NS4wLjA.

emotionally withdrawn, unresponsive, or detached. Neither is good for children.

Bear in mind that distress is not the opposite of stress—it's worse. It's normal for parents to worry about their child's development, behavior, and safety throughout their lives. Additionally, the never-ending list of tasks and responsibilities can feel overwhelming. However, when these daily stresses become too much to handle, they can transform into chronic anxiety or severe depression, making parents question their ability to fulfill their roles. This state is known as distress.

Addressing mental health issues with a therapist or doctor is crucial for being an effective parent. If feelings of sadness persist, it's important to watch for symptoms of depression, which include:

- Hopelessness
- Loss of interest in hobbies
- Difficulty concentrating (mental fog)
- Irritability
- Insomnia
- Suicidal thoughts

Seeking professional help can provide the support needed to manage these symptoms and improve parenting skills.

By understanding how stress affects parenting and the various factors that contribute to it, parents can better navigate the challenges of raising children. Implementing effective stress management strategies and seeking support when needed can help create a healthier and more positive environment for both you and your children.

You'll likely worry about your child's development, behavior, and safety their whole life. But if your day-to-day becomes overwhelming, your feelings may transform into chronic anxiety or debilitating depression that causes you to question your ability as a parent. In this case, you might be distressed.

Addressing your mental health with a therapist or doctor is the best way to show up for your child.

THE GENETICS OF PARENTING

Parents bring a variety of traits and qualities to the parenting relationship that influences their decisions and behaviors. These characteristics include a parent's age, gender identity, personality, developmental history, beliefs, knowledge about parenting and child development, and mental and physical health. Personality traits significantly affect parenting behaviors. For example, parents who are more agreeable, conscientious, and outgoing tend to be warmer and provide more structure for their children. Similarly, parents who are agreeable, less anxious, and less negative are better at supporting their children's autonomy compared to parents who are anxious and less agreeable.

This is where genes come in. While it may seem that these attitudes shape the child's emotional development, traits like conscientiousness and agreeableness are heavily mediated by genes.[8]So, it may be that the children have simply inherited their parents' attitudes biologically. This is also why getting angry at your child doesn't affect their long-term outcomes.

---

8. Kendra Cherry, "How Personality Traits Are Developed and Change Over Time," Verywell Mind, March 1, 2023, https://www.verywellmind.com/are-personality-traits-caused-by-genes-or-environment-4120707.

Nonetheless, insensitive parenting behaviors are associated with lower levels of kind and prosocial behavior in school-aged children. In contrast, warm, sensitive, and responsive caregiving can increase a child's oxytocin levels and positively influence a child's overall health and development. This shows how parental stress can negatively impact a child's development, with researchers identifying several mechanisms. For instance, distressed parents might serve as poor role models, with children observing and mimicking their negative behaviors.

Observational studies tracking families over the years have found evidence for bidirectional effects between parenting stress and child behavior problems. Essentially, challenging child behaviors can increase parental stress, which in turn can exacerbate the child's behavior problems.[9]

However, bear in mind that research has consistently shown that children in stressful environments are at risk of developing behavioral and emotional problems. For example, parental anxiety and household stress have been linked to children's emotional and behavioral issues, including aggression, anxiety, and depression. Additionally, maternal stress in infancy can predict later anxiety in children, particularly if the child has a difficult or negative temperament. Maternal anxiety and depression are also associated with children's impulsiveness and attention problems.

Understanding the multifaceted impact of parental stress is crucial for addressing and mitigating its effects on children's health and development. By learning how to deal with anger arising from

9. Shou-Chun Chiang and Sunhye Bai, "Bidirectional Associations between Parenting Stress and Child Psychopathology: The Moderating Role of Maternal Affection," *Development and Psychopathology*, September 29, 2023, 1–11, https://doi.org/10.1017/S0954579423001177.

stress, you will make your parenting experience and your children's relationship with you much better,

In the next chapter, you will get a toolkit to achieve this.

2

INTRODUCTION TO THE C.A.L.M.S. ANGER MANAGEMENT TOOLKIT

> *If you're not yelling at your kids, you aren't spending enough time with them.*
>
> — MARK RUFFALO, ACTOR

E ven if you aren't by nature a hot-tempered person, the many responsibilities you juggle as a parent—maintaining a job and putting Jimmy to sleep, managing household finances and helping Jimmy color inside the lines, completing chores and taking the toy car out of Jimmy's left nostril, running errands and running after Jimmy as he bolts out the front door—can leave you feeling stressed and overwhelmed. This makes it harder to stay patient and calm, even if Jimmy finds it all great fun.

Disagreements over parenting styles, discipline, or the division of household chores create tension and frustration. Moreover, work-related stress, lack of sleep, fatigue, health issues, and financial concerns make it that much harder to maintain patience and composure when dealing with Jimmy's constant demands.

The fact that you're reading this book means that you often get angry with your child. More importantly, it also means that you feel bad about getting angry with them. No doubt you've tried to get a handle on your outbursts and failed or at least not been as successful as you would like. (Full disclosure: This is also why I wrote the book.)

This chapter provides techniques and tips to reach these goals. We apply what is called the C.A.L.M.S. approach, which stands for Comprehend Your Triggers, Always Stay Calm, Leverage Communication, Maintain Positivity, and Seek Support. (Yes, we only use strategies that have a cute acronym.)

TRIGGER WARNING: THIS SECTION DESCRIBES TRIGGERS

You can't stop getting angry unless you know what gets you angry. This might seem obvious, yet most people don't realize this. That's because anger, by its very nature, prevents clear thinking. Worse yet, we unconsciously see anger as justified—the term "righteous anger" is redundant because, at least in the moment, we always view our anger as righteous. Since anger is often triggered by situations that we consider unfair or unwarranted, we don't spend much time anticipating such situations and preparing to control ourselves when they arise.

With respect to your child, common triggers are lack of cooperation, disregarding instructions, rudeness, defiance, behaving badly in front of other people, and even doing a task slowly or poorly.[1] Do any of these sound familiar? If not, then I'm afraid your child is

---

1. Beth Sissons, "Anger Management for Parents: Causes of Anger and How to Control It," February 24, 2022 https://www.medicalnewstoday.com/articles/anger-management-for-parents.

not your biological offspring. They're an angel sent by God Almighty Himself.

Recognizing your initial trigger, or "hook," is the first step in managing your emotions as a parent. This trigger could be your child's perceived disrespect or misbehavior, your partner neglecting a task, or a loud sibling argument. This last is my particular trigger. I have two children, and I get most angry at both of them when they bully the other.

Identifying your triggers/hooks allows you to regulate your emotions more quickly. Notice the trigger by paying attention to your physical symptoms, such as a racing heart or a knotted stomach. Then do this: pause and take a breath. If you miss it in the moment, reflect on the episode afterward to identify your triggers.

Seven Anger Control Strategies

1. Recognize early signs of anger, such as feelings of irritation, annoyance, muscle tension, a racing heartbeat, rapid breathing, sweating, or negative thoughts. Identifying these signs allows you to take proactive steps to calm down.
2. Inform your child that you are starting to feel angry and need a moment to cool down. This communication helps both you and your child learn about emotional regulation.
3. Focus on deep breathing: inhale slowly and deeply, then exhale with a sigh, repeating until calm.
4. Slowly count to ten, and repeat, if necessary, to defuse anger.
5. If possible, remove yourself from the stressful situation for a longer period. Taking a warm shower, stepping outside for fresh air, or finding a quiet space to be alone can help.

6. Engage in physical activities like running, gardening, cleaning, or working on a house project to channel anger into productive energy.
7. Find joy and relaxation in activities like painting, listening to music, or reading a book or magazine.
8. Put your child up for adoption.

Okay, I'm kidding with that last one. (Really!) And, since none of us want to give the little rascals away, it's better to recognize the signs of anger and employ various calming techniques. This helps prevent anger from negatively impacting your interactions with your children and creates a more peaceful home environment.

Taking proactive steps to control your anger can also help you cope with guilt and other feelings. Practicing self-compassion and acknowledging that factors like lack of sleep and work stress affect your emotions are also important.

If you have lost your temper with your children, discussing the incident with them and explaining the reasons behind your anger can be constructive. Remember: Apologize for losing your temper, not for being angry. As I noted in the Introduction, anger is a natural and common emotion and is not inherently negative. It is how you express anger that matters.

Additionally, you can show your children what a more appropriate response would have been, such as taking a moment to calm down. This approach not only addresses the immediate issue but also teaches your children healthier ways to manage their own anger.

BREATHING CAN SAVE YOUR (FAMILY) LIFE

As you acknowledge your thoughts and emotions, focus on your breathing. Top athletes and performers and Stormy Daniels emphasize the importance of the exhale. Aim to make your exhalations as long as possible, concentrating on creating space rather than eliminating stress. This can help you maintain calm and composure, allowing for more thoughtful responses to the situation.

By following these steps, you can better manage your emotional responses, fostering a healthier and more supportive environment for your children. Recognizing triggers, pausing to understand your reactions, and focusing on controlled breathing are key strategies in regulating emotions and improving your interactions with your family.

Close your eyes or rest your gaze. Slowly inhale through your nose while counting to four, focusing on the air entering your lungs. Engage your senses by paying attention to the feeling and sounds of your breathing. Gently hold your breath for a count of four, avoiding any inhalation or exhalation. Then, begin to slowly exhale through your nose for four seconds. Repeat these steps at least three times.

For a more intense practice, try increasing the count to 4-7-8: Inhale for a count of four, gently hold for a count of seven, and exhale for a count of eight. If your stress response is very intense, deep breathing might initially cause more stress. In such cases, physical movement can help—try walking, doing push-ups, or running up the stairs to offload cortisol and adrenaline before attempting deep breathing again. Use your breath to help release these stress hormones.

Connect with your body by grounding yourself. Push your feet into the floor as if it's sand on a beach. (Between the soothing sound of the waves, the relaxing brush of the wind, and the ice-cold beers in the cooler, it's harder to get angry by the sea. Unless you have a child who screams when they get sand between their toes.)

A very useful technique in the heat of anger is to connect with your values to guide your behavior.[2] I find this useful, not just for anger but for stress in general. Reflect on the kind of parent you want to be in the moment. Remember, you cannot control the thoughts, feelings, or behaviors of others. You might influence them when you are calm, but not when you are out of control. The only thing you can control is your behavior—how you choose to respond. Anger can make you feel powerful and energized, which is useful in social conflict (once you direct and control it—bulging forehead veins and spittle, intimidating though they may be, are not useful tools for getting one's way).

If you lose control initially and yell at your child or lash out, remember that you have acted contrary to your values. When you recognize this, own your mistake, commit to improving, and communicate this to your child. You might say, "Sorry that I reacted that way. I'll work on it. What did you need from me then?" This approach not only helps you align with your values but also teaches your child about accountability and growth.

WHY WORRY? BECAUSE I'M A PARENT, DUH

If, as a parent, you don't worry, you're probably not doing it right. On the other hand, if you do worry, you're probably not doing it right, either. So, the first step in relieving stress is to not worry about worrying.

---

2. Jan Newman, "6 Steps to Emotional Self-Awareness for Parents" *Https://Momentumpsychology.Com/* (blog), May 19, 2021 https://momentumpsychology.com/6stepsemotional-awareness/.

Here are parents' four most common concerns:

1. Your child will be hurt, unloved, or mistreated by fate or friends.
2. Things don't go as planned or envisioned.
3. Your child's demands exceed your current skills or resources.
4. You experience setbacks, failures, and unmet expectations for your child.

Amidst all the challenges, listen to your inner voice. During tough parenting moments, this inner voice often acts as a harsh critic, constantly judging, condemning, and predicting negative outcomes. Its incessant chatter makes parenting more difficult than necessary. Therefore, it's essential to set aside time to compassionately examine and create space around this internal parental critic.

Through dedicated mindfulness practices, you can train your anxious-prone mind to remain present and observant amid the fluctuations of your mental and emotional experiences, patiently awaiting the transformation of pain. See your mind as a puppy in training, without the peeing. With consistent mindfulness practice, you can cultivate resilience, learning to endure discomfort without succumbing to prolonged suffering.

MIND THE PARENT

Self-awareness is crucial because it involves understanding yourself clearly, recognizing how others perceive you, and understanding your role in society and the world. One study found that individuals who practiced self-reflection and had high self-awareness often possessed a more positive self-image and a deeper understanding of others, leading to greater empathy.[3]

People with higher self-awareness are also typically more proactive in their work environment and exhibit better communication skills. The positive traits associated with high self-awareness can enhance overall well-being.

When faced with pain, whether physical or emotional, it's beneficial to have developed the ability to mindfully observe it, allowing it to exist without resistance and witnessing it as it naturally evolves and often diminishes over time. Attempting to forcefully push away or suppress pain often leads it to linger and intensify, becoming a constant companion to the mind—i.e., suffering.

You can learn to "rest" within the experience of pain without exacerbating it with the mind's anxieties and agendas. This practice is commonly known in mindfulness as "acceptance." However, acceptance does not imply resignation or surrendering to the pain of parenting. Rather, it involves an active and empowered choice to recline and allow the pain to flow through you. What's essential is to take a "N.A.P." with the pain that arises in your daily life as a parent. Here are the steps:

- **Notice:** Observe and acknowledge the painful sensations in your body and any accompanying thoughts that arise.
- **Allow:** Permit everything to be as it is, refraining from attempting to alter or suppress anything.
- **Pass:** Allow the pain to pass through you, resting in the present moment until the painful thoughts and feelings naturally dissipate.

---

3. Anna Sutton, "Measuring the Effects of Self-Awareness: Construction of the Self-Awareness Outcomes Questionnaire," *Europe's Journal of Psychology* 12, no. 4 (November 2016): 645–58, https://doi.org/10.5964/ejop.v12i4.1178.

With consistent practice, you'll develop the ability to take a "nap" even during louder, more intense, or historically challenging episodes. Be patient with yourself. Remember, the struggles of parenting are universal, and no one is immune. We're all on this journey together, striving for greater mindfulness in our relationships with our children. This journey is called "practice," emphasizing progress over perfection.

Many parents strive to practice mindful parenting, aiming to be fully present with their children, devoid of distractions or judgment, and with a compassionate and receptive mindset. While this aspiration may sound simple, it's often challenging to implement consistently. However, the outcome of providing such focused attention is profound: We become more attentive, aware, kind, and understanding in our interactions with our children. When managing tasks, we learn to tackle one thing at a time, moment by moment, task by task.

Mindful parenting involves setting a continual intention to be present in the moment. This presence can manifest in various ways, such as actively listening to your child, recognizing your own emotions during conflicts, pausing before reacting, and acknowledging your child's perspectives, even if they differ from your own.[4]

In essence, mindful parenting entails pausing to attune to your child's deeper needs—whether they are hungry, sleepy, scared, or experiencing other emotions—and responding to them thoughtfully and compassionately. By applying mindfulness principles to parenthood, we create opportunities to be more responsive, productive, and less overwhelmed, moving away from autopilot mode.

---

4. Headspace, "What is mindful parenting?" Retrieved 29/05/24, https://www.headspace.com/mindfulness/mindful-parenting.

While striving to be a mindful parent may seem daunting amidst the daily stresses of family life, breaking down the day into manageable segments and progressing step by step helps train the mind to be more present. Research indicates that parents who practice mindful parenting exhibit more positive and less negative parenting behaviors, leading to positive outcomes in their children, such as reduced anxiety, depression, and behavioral issues.

Use the STOP method—Stop, Take (a breath), Observe, and Proceed. This can help you create mindful pauses in your interactions with your child. These practices facilitate clearer, calmer responses from a more centered mental state, fostering healthier parent-child relationships.

Once you've practiced these techniques, you can expect the following benefits:

- **Improved Emotional Regulation**: Recognize emotional triggers and respond calmly, modeling effective emotion management for children.
- **Increased Patience**: Encourage pausing before reacting, fostering patience and understanding.
- **Enhanced Communication**: Actively listen to create an environment for open dialogue.
- **Strengthened Bond**: Emphasize quality time and attentiveness, strengthening the parent-child relationship.
- **Reduced Stress**: Focus on the present moment, reducing stress and anxiety.
- **Decreased Reactivity**: Promote thoughtful responses over knee-jerk reactions.

- **Self-Compassion**: Recognize parenting challenges, promoting well-being and self-care.[5]

In the next chapter, we embark on a deeper exploration of identifying and managing your emotional triggers.

---

5. Chris Mosunic, "Mindful Parenting: What It Is, benefits & 10 Ways to Practice," Calm, May 5, 2024.

3

THE AWESOMENESS OF AWARENESS

> *Never raise your hand to your kids. It leaves your groin unprotected.*

— RED BUTTONS, ACTOR

Here's something I bet most men had to do when they became dads: stop swearing.

I certainly did. Before my daughter was born, I cursed like a nineteenth-century sailor. (I assume the twenty-first-century seamen have been given sensitivity training so they don't traumatize the polar bears.)

Anyway, I used to swear a lot while driving. Also, while playing hockey, baking turkey, and having sex (this last one was only when requested, though). When I was a teenager, I read a quote (I think) from Mark Twain, which said, "In certain circumstances, profanity affords a relief denied even to prayer." And I didn't grow up to be a praying man. Then, my daughter was born and was often present when I was driving or cooking. (I no longer had time for hockey, baking, or sex.) So now, when I was in the car or the kitchen and some mishap happened, I had to always remember that children are sponges, and I didn't want my daughter's first words to be "F***ing moron!"

That was the start of my new self-awareness as a parent.

This chapter will, I hope, give you a deeper understanding of self-awareness so you can more effectively manage your reactions as a parent. You'll get all the tools you need to understand your emotional patterns, implement regular self-reflection, and manage stress to become a more mindful and effective parent.

We focus here on the C component of the C.A.L.M.S. Anger Management Toolkit: comprehend your triggers. Strategy 1 (recognizing triggers) and Strategy 2 (stress management techniques) will help you learn to identify personal triggers and implement stress reduction strategies, enhancing emotional self-regulation.

SELF-AWARENESS: THE ULTIMATE PARENTING TOOL

I didn't really start using the techniques in this book until my daughter was two years old. I think that was also around the time my wife and I started being intimate again. (Much of that period remains a blur, but I assume we were having more "private time" because my son was born a year later.)

When my wife became pregnant for the second time, I was a conceited father. I had learned to feed my daughter, play peeka-boo, and, yes, change diapers. (See my book, 7 Chapters Every First Time Dad Needs to Read.) I was also able to cajole her into doing things (or, rather, not doing things), like not taking off her dress as soon as we put it on, not splashing all the water out of the bathtub, not jumping on Mommy's stomach when she found out her brother was in there. (Yes, sibling rivalry started early in our family.)

So, all in all, I was a much calmer parent than my wife, and I expected to be even calmer when my son came along.

Little did I know.

What I found out the first week he was born was that my daughter had been an angel. She cried only when she needed to be fed, cleaned, or put to sleep. He cried for all those things, plus other stuff we never figured out. Was the light in the bedroom too bright? Too dim? Too electric? Apart from that, he didn't sleep for even two hours, as my daughter had. He woke up at all times, fed on no schedule at all, and threw up constantly. We carried him to the pediatrician constantly, only to be told each time he was a healthy, normal baby. That's when I realized doctors are just making it up as they go along.

My nerves were frayed, and, let me confess, I even ended up shouting a few times at my newborn son. I realized I needed to get a handle on my emotions. So, I followed the oldest and most important rule of psychology: Know thyself.

Self-awareness is super important for any parent because it helps create a healthy emotional environment for your whole family. When you understand your own emotions, you can keep the home more stable and supportive, which is great for everyone's well-being.

Being self-aware also means you can act with intention. By knowing your own emotional triggers, you can respond to situations more thoughtfully. This means your actions are more in line with what your family needs, leading to better and healthier interactions.

Knowing and managing emotions is another big benefit of self-awareness. When you understand your feelings, you can handle stress better and improve the overall family dynamics. This emotional understanding helps keep things balanced and harmonious at home.

Practicing self-awareness also helps you teach your kids to understand and manage their emotions. When they see you being aware and in control of your feelings, they learn to do the same. This helps them develop their own emotional intelligence, making it easier for them to deal with their feelings as they grow. According to Harvard's National Scientific Council on the Developing Child, the brain's ability to adapt, known as plasticity, is highest in early childhood and decreases with age. As the brain matures and becomes more specialized, it stabilizes and becomes less flexible. This means that the earlier you start nurturing your child's development, the more effective it will be in shaping their future abilities and responses.[1]

As I mentioned in Chapter Two (and I'm repeating it here because it's so important), the first step here is figuring out your parenting triggers. In parenting, a trigger is when your child does something that suddenly makes you feel very angry, hurt, or helpless. When your child gets upset and you respond with anger or annoyance at their whining, tantrums, or crying, it's often more about your own difficulties processing these emotions than the child's behavior.

Triggers can interfere with your ability to effectively and positively parent your children. Instead of reacting calmly and supportively when your kids are upset or facing challenges, you might find yourself yelling, getting short with them, telling them to stop

---

1. Center on the Developing Child at Harvard University, "Center on the Developing Child at Harvard University," Accessed January 6, 2024, https://developingchild.harvard.edu/.

crying, or threatening time-outs. These reactions often aim to lessen your own emotional discomfort rather than being the best way to help your kids.

It's essential to recognize when you've been triggered. Here are seven clues to help you identify when this happens:

1. **Excessive Anger**: If you find yourself excessively angry at your kids, yelling at the top of your lungs with sweaty palms and a red face, you've definitely been triggered.
2. **Deep Sadness or Hurt**: When you feel deeply sad, upset, or hurt by something your child said or did, even though you know you shouldn't take it personally, you've probably been triggered.
3. **Out of Proportion Reactions**: If your feelings of upset, fear, or anger are out of proportion to the situation, which you realize after you cool down, you've probably been triggered.
4. **Feeling Out of Control**: If you feel like your reactions are out of your control, you've definitely been triggered.
5. **Familiar Feelings**: If you feel like you've experienced this kind of feeling many times before, and it feels very familiar, you've been triggered.
6. **Sudden Intense Feelings**: If your feelings seem to come out of nowhere, going from calm to extremely angry in seconds, you've been triggered.
7. **Physical Aggression**: If you find yourself suddenly wanting to grab, slap, spank, or otherwise physically hurt your child, you've definitely been triggered.[2]

---

2. Sue Lively, "What You NEED to Know About Parenting Triggers" *One Time Through* (blog), May 31, 2015 https://onetimethrough.com/what-you-need-to-know-about-parenting-triggers/.

Often, you need to take a step back and analyze the situation before reacting. This helps you recognize your triggers and allows you to respond more proactively. By identifying your parenting triggers, you can uncover the roots of past emotional wounds that affect your relationship with your child.

We all have our own issues, but understanding your triggers is the first step to emotional and mental healing. The key to identifying your parenting triggers is to pay attention to your feelings and look for patterns in your reactions.

MOOD OF THE DAY

It can be hard to keep track of your feelings. It can even be counterproductive. For men, it's onerous because we don't think our feelings need to be thought about. It's the same for women since whatever they feel must be correct and justified, and who are you to tell me what to feel anyway?

This is why I found it useful to keep a mood diary. I'd set aside ten minutes at the end of the day to record what I recalled about my emotions throughout the day. Then, at the end of the week, I'd go through my entries, making notes on what I needed to change and how to do so.

Mood charts help track when, where, and how often certain moods are experienced and expressed. By collecting enough data, patterns of highs and lows can be identified, along with factors that may have triggered them.

A mood chart is particularly useful for individuals with depression, bipolar disorder, and anxiety. However, anyone seeking to understand themselves better can benefit from this tool. It provides valuable insights into mood fluctuations, helping you take proactive steps toward self-awareness and self-control.

When it comes to feelings, it's useful to understand the three categories they fall into: affect, emotions, and mood:

Affect refers to our overall feelings experienced throughout our days, weeks, and months.

Emotions are responses to specific events or situations.

Moods are the background feelings that accompany us without any particular reason or cause.

Psychologists define mood as persistent feelings that accompany our perception and evaluation of incoming stimuli. Mood significantly influences how we react and the feelings that arise throughout that process.

Unlike emotions, which stem from specific events, moods represent our overall state and can last much longer. They can come and go without warning, cause, or reason, making them tricky to track.

Personality plays a role in how moods are displayed and how people act during different phases. Optimistic individuals tend to gather more positive information from their surroundings, maintaining a positive affect. Pessimistic individuals, on the other hand, may seek evidence to support their negative state, reinforcing their negative feelings.

This feedback loop can strengthen negative thoughts, leading to prolonged negative experiences. Without a balanced view of the environment, a biased and subjective mental state can persist. This is where mood charts become valuable.

A 10-STEP PLAN TO MANAGE YOUR MOODS

Once you've started to understand yourself better, the following steps will help you gain more control over your anger and stress:

1. **Start with Self-Compassion**: Avoid judging yourself harshly when negative thoughts about your child arise. Guilt often leads to overcompensation and resentment. Instead of pushing these feelings away, take a moment to understand them without labeling them. Ask yourself why you feel upset with your child's behavior, and address your worries calmly. By doing so, you can find solutions that benefit both you and your child, breaking the cycle of remorse.

2. **Understand Child Development**: Learn about the emotional characteristics of different developmental stages. Knowing what to expect helps you empathize with your child's feelings and respond with patience. For instance, toddlers' tantrums are part of asserting independence, while preschoolers may struggle with separation anxiety. Educating yourself on these stages helps you navigate emotional situations effectively.

3. **Manage Expectations**: Set realistic expectations for yourself and your child. Parenting has its highs and lows, and it's okay not to handle every situation perfectly. Accept that there will be challenges, and reflect on your reactions to improve future responses. Additionally, understand what behaviors are typical for your child's age and adjust your expectations accordingly.

4. **Practice Mindfulness**: Stay grounded in the present moment and aware of your thoughts and emotions. Mindfulness helps you avoid reacting impulsively to parenting stress. Incorporate mindfulness into your daily

routine through meditation or breathing exercises. Engage your child in kid-friendly mindfulness activities to teach them emotional regulation skills.

5. **Prioritize Physical Activity**: Regular exercise boosts your mood and resilience, making it easier to handle parenting challenges. Schedule time for physical activity each day, even if it's just a short walk. Make exercise a family activity to promote bonding and stress relief. Staying active ensures you approach parenting moments with positivity and energy.

6. **Practice Gratitude**: Focus on the positives in your life, even during challenging times. Reflect on what you're grateful for each day to shift your perspective. Express gratitude to your child and partner to foster connection and appreciation. Gratitude helps you approach parenting with patience and compassion.

7. **Use Positive Affirmations**: Combat negative self-talk with affirmations that reinforce your strengths as a parent. Repeat affirmations to yourself during difficult moments to boost your confidence and resilience. Share affirmations with loved ones to uplift each other and build a supportive community.

8. **Prioritize Self-Care**: Make time for relaxation and joy to recharge your emotional reserves. Schedule regular self-care activities like reading or spending time outdoors. Seek support from friends, family, or online parenting groups when needed. Remember that taking care of yourself enables you to be a better parent to your child.

9. **Establish a Support System**: Connect with others who can offer understanding and guidance in your parenting journey. Lean on friends, family, or support groups to share experiences and seek advice. Communicate openly

with your partner about your feelings and collaborate on parenting challenges.

10. **Seek Professional Help**: If you struggle to regulate your emotions consistently, consider seeking therapy or counseling. A mental health professional can help you address underlying issues and develop healthy coping strategies. Don't hesitate to reach out for support when needed—it's a proactive step toward better emotional well-being for you and your child.[3]

IT'S ALL IN YOUR MIND

Two basic stress relaxation techniques are muscle relaxation and visualization. I've found both very useful and, unlike the Downward Facing Dog Backward Wag Tail yoga, very easy to do.

Start by finding a comfortable position, either lying down or sitting. Take a moment to relax your entire body, and then take five deep, slow breaths.

- Lift your toes upward, holding for a moment and releasing. Then, pull your toes downward, hold briefly, and release.
- Tense your calf muscles, then release.
- Move your knees toward each other, hold briefly, and then release.
- Squeeze your thigh muscles, hold for a moment, and then release.
- Clench your hands into fists, pause, and then release.
- Tense your arms, hold briefly, and then release.

---

3. Tali Shenfield, "13 Ways To Manage And Control Your Emotions And Become A Better Parent," Child Psychology Resources by Dr. Tali Shenfield, February 8, 2020, https://www.psy-ed.com/wpblog/manage-your-emotions/.

- Squeeze your buttocks, pause, and then release.
- Contract your abdominal muscles, pause, and then release.
- Inhale deeply and tighten your chest, hold briefly, then exhale and release.
- Raise your shoulders toward your ears, pause, and then release.
- Press your lips together tightly, hold, and then release.
- Open your mouth wide, hold, and then release.
- Close your eyes tightly, pause, and then release.
- Lift your eyebrows, hold, and then release.

The guided imagery exercise is just as simple. First, find a comfortable spot to sit or lie down. Close your eyes and take a few deep breaths to begin relaxing your body.

Visualization entails sitting or lying comfortably and imagining any scene you find relaxing. It could be the sea, a waterfall, a forest, a child-proof study. Imagine this scene vividly, adding details like the sounds of birds chirping, the fragrance of flowers, the warmth of the sun, and a silent child. Spend a few minutes in this imagined setting, soaking in the peacefulness and relaxation. Stay in the scene for as long as needed to feel rejuvenated.

When ready, gently open your eyes and stretch to return to the present moment. Remember that you can revisit this calming scene whenever desired.

REFLECT ON YOUR REFLECTION

Positive parenting offers numerous advantages, but it requires a lot of time, the patience of Job, significant effort, and many drugs you should never take. Since the outcomes are not immediate, taking a moment for self-reflection can help you stay focused during tough times and maintain your sanity. Self-reflection might not be a habit many of us are accustomed to, but here are some tips to start integrating it into your daily life:

Start Journaling

Dedicate five to ten minutes each day to jot down your thoughts and feelings, either with pen and paper or using the notes app on your phone. You can use journaling prompts or simply write about a particular situation or behavior your child is exhibiting. For instance, if you've been dealing with bedtime battles with your toddler and feeling frustrated, take some time after your child goes to bed to reflect. Ask yourself questions like what happens before bedtime? How do I feel in the afternoon? How does my tone of voice affect the situation? How does my child respond to my emotions? Make sure you find some alone time to give this exercise the attention it deserves. And who knows? You might find you've written the next big comedy (or, depending on your child, drama).

Pay Attention to Your Immediate Situation

Amid daily chaos, it's easy to ignore our feelings, only to realize later that we're too exhausted to address them. While it may not be feasible to pause during a challenging parenting moment, try to find a few minutes afterward to reflect on your thoughts and emotions about the situation. Jot down your feelings as soon as possible after they occur, as this will help you remember them more accurately and work on them later. If you're unable to stop and write, use the voice memo app on your phone to record your thoughts.

Find Some Alone Time

While it's challenging to carve out alone time, it's essential for reflection. Alone time doesn't necessarily mean being completely by yourself; it simply means having time to think. Use moments like your child's nap or a short stroller walk to and from the park to be present with your thoughts and emotions without distractions like podcasts, social media, or memories of how easy life was before you were a parent. Disconnecting from devices allows you to reconnect with yourself. If you already have some alone time in your daily routine, such as during a workout, incorporate self-reflection into that time. Make the most of the alone time you have, whether it's existing or newly created.

Consider Self-Reflection Questions

Using prompts can help stimulate your thoughts and feelings during self-reflection. Remember, the goal is not to criticize yourself but to be mindful of your feelings and desires in your parenting journey.[4]

Here are some suggested self-reflection questions. Choose the ones that you think will be most useful to you.

1. What values do I hope my children will embody as adults?
2. What kind of parent do I aspire to be?
3. Which parenting approach feels most natural and comfortable for me?
4. Am I prioritizing my own well-being and needs?

---

4. Camila Martelo, "What Is Positive Parenting Self-Reflection?" October 17, 2023, https://huckleberrycare.com/blog/what-is-positive-parenting-self-reflection.

5. Are there particular stressors that impact my parenting abilities?
6. How effectively are my partner and I collaborating to achieve our desired parenting style?
7. What resources or strategies consistently support me as a parent?

Self-reflection questions for specific parenting incidents or behaviors:

1. What was my emotional state leading up to this situation?
2. Is this behavior a one-time occurrence or a recurring pattern?
3. Do I notice any consistent patterns in this behavior?
4. Could this behavior be triggered by an unmet need, such as hunger or fatigue?
5. How do I feel when my child behaves this way?
6. How do I ideally want to respond when my child behaves like this?
7. What actions can I take now to prevent or address this behavior in the future for both me and my child?

The following step-by-step emotional awareness plan will make it easier to implement the advice from this chapter.

1. **Recording Stressful Moments**:
   - **Step**: Over the course of a week, jot down instances where you feel stressed or angry. Note the situation, your emotions, and what you believe triggered your reaction.
   - **Purpose**: This exercise aids in identifying recurring emotional patterns and pinpointing specific triggers within your parenting environment.

2. **Recognizing Emotional Patterns**:
   - **Step**: Each night, reflect on occasions when you felt overwhelmed or had strong reactions. Identify the emotion and the thoughts that came before it.
   - **Purpose**: Understanding your emotional patterns enables you to foresee and prepare for situations that might provoke negative responses.
3. **Daily Self-Reflection**:
   - **Step**: Allocate ten minutes daily for self-reflection. Ponder on moments when you handled your emotions effectively and areas where you could have improved.
   - **Purpose**: Consistent self-reflection fosters emotional insight and facilitates the integration of healthier response patterns.
4. **Role-Playing with Family**:
   - **Step**: Engage in role-playing sessions with your partner or a friend, acting out scenarios that typically trigger you. Experiment with various ways to manage your reactions.
   - **Purpose**: Role-playing serves as preparation for real-life situations, boosting confidence in managing them adeptly.
5. **Developing a Trigger Management Plan**:
   - **Step**: Utilizing insights from your journal and role-playing, devise a management strategy for addressing known triggers. This may involve techniques like deep breathing, using calming phrases, or temporarily stepping away from the situation to regain composure.
   - **Purpose**: Having a pre-established plan enhances your ability to handle triggers constructively as they arise.

By implementing these steps, you can apply the calming techniques outlined in the following chapter to real-life scenarios. This will foster better interactions and relationships with your child. Each step offers actionable strategies with tools to effectively manage your emotional responses.

4

ALWAYS STAY CALM

> *You can learn many things from children. How much patience you have, for instance.*
>
> — FRANKLIN P. JONES (AMERICAN BUSINESSMAN AND HUMORIST)

I first learned about mindful parenting through one of my wife's friends, who I will call Brittany. Like us, Brittany was in her early thirties, juggling the demands of raising two young children, ages seven and five, while managing a career. Her husband had to travel a lot for work, so she had more responsibilities than in our household, where my wife and I divvied up the child-care tasks. At one point, Brittany confided to my wife that the never-ending cycle of school runs, work responsibilities, deadlines, household chores, and even playtime left her feeling overwhelmed and stressed.

Then, within a few months, we saw a change. Even though she was still doing the same routine, she seemed calmer and more good-tempered every time we met her. At the time, I was working on my second book, *The First Time Dad's Guide to Raising a Toddler*, and I asked her how she was coping so well.

It turned out that, looking for help, Brittany had stumbled upon the concept of mindful parenting and decided to give it a try. Starting small, she incorporated mindfulness into her daily routine, taking deep breaths during chaotic moments and consciously engaging with her children. Later, she went to a mindful parenting workshop.

To her surprise, the effects were profound. She told us that as she practiced being present and calm, she noticed a shift in her mood and demeanor. Best of all, her children, sensing the change, responded with newfound cooperation and affection.

With each mindful interaction, Brittany said she felt more connected to her children and herself. Her previously stressful household was transformed into a haven of love and understanding. This showed that the simplest practices can yield the greatest rewards.

My wife and I then started to research mindful parenting and use some of the techniques.

This chapter shows you how to integrate mindfulness into parenting. This will enhance your well-being and family relationships. You will learn how to incorporate mindfulness practices into your parenting style. You will be able to use these techniques to stay calm and engaged with your children. This will foster more considerate interactions and reduce guilt-driven outbursts. You will develop a more thoughtful and present mindset.

We accomplish all this under the "A" component of the C.A.L.M.S. Anger Management Toolkit. We use Strategy 3 (deep breathing exercises), Strategy 4 (mindfulness practices and strategy), and Strategy 5 (creating calm spaces at home).

Nothing worthwhile is achieved without effort. In this chapter, the hard work begins. The good news is that once you regularly practice the exercises described here, they will become second nature. This will benefit you not only as a parent but in life as a whole. You will find yourself less stressed, less angry, and better at handling the daily obstacles we all encounter as we go through our day.

PRESENT PARENT

Mindful parenting means always trying to be present. This can mean paying attention to your child, noticing your feelings during conflicts, pausing before reacting, and listening to your child's viewpoints, even if they are different from yours. In short, mindful parenting means pausing to understand your child's needs (like if they are crying because they are hungry, tired, scared, or something else) and responding with care and love.

These are the benefits of becoming a mindful parent:

- You'll respond better to your kids and feel less stressed.
- You will learn to pause, stop multitasking, and live in the moment.
- Your children will feel calmer.[1]

---

1. Headspace, "What is mindful parenting?" Retrieved 29/05/24, https://www.headspace.com/mindfulness/mindful-parenting.

Many parents try to practice mindful parenting by being fully present with their children without distractions or judgment. This is hard to do, but it helps us be more attentive, aware, kind, and understanding with our children. When we do tasks, we focus on one thing at a time, moment by moment.

Okay, I know what you're thinking: "I don't have the time or energy to think all day." You're right. Me, neither. The trick is to break your day into manageable parts. Do one task at a time. This helps train our minds to be more present. When that mindset becomes second nature, it brings calm, clarity, and a more positive perspective.

Yes, it still requires considerable work to achieve this. But the benefits for our kids are worth the effort. The research shows that mindful parenting helps parents handle conflicts calmly and kindly, and it also helps kids behave better with less anxiety, depression, and acting out.

One study[2] found that parents who practiced mindful parenting had more positive interactions with their kids, which led to better behavior. Parents showed less negative emotion and shared more positive feelings with their adolescent children, which was linked to lower drug use in the teens.

So, let's go a bit deeper into mindfulness.

HOW TO TRAIN YOUR MIND

When my wife and I first went to a mindful parenting workshop, I was surprised to see that there were a lot more women than men

2. Justin Parent, Laura G. McKee, Jennifer N. Rough, and Rex Forehand, "The Association of Parent Mindfulness with Parenting and Youth Psychopathology Across Three Developmental Stages," *Journal of Abnormal Child Psychology* 44, no. 1 (January 2016): 191–202, https://doi.org/10.1007/s10802-015-9978-x.

there. Later, when I thought about it, I was surprised at my surprise.

I had unconsciously assumed that there would be as many, if not more, dads than moms at a parenting workshop that dealt with self-control. This is because I had made two assumptions: (1) that men are more prone to anger than women, and (2) that men need more help being dads than women do being moms.

The first is true, but men more often direct their anger at objects, issues, other men, and their spouses. And that last is generally superseded by the instinct to protect. As for parent-child relationships, while dads may not be as emotionally expressive as moms to their children, that's a double-edged sword. Several studies show that mothers get angry more often and more intensely at their children than fathers do.[3] To be sure, this is partly explained by the fact that mothers spend more time caring for their children than fathers. But the fact remains that moms need mindfulness more to help deal with their stress and anger.

Let's begin with five basic steps for practicing mindfulness in your daily life:

1. **Make time for it**. You don't need any special equipment; just set aside some time and find a quiet space.

---

3. See Nelson, J. A., O'Brien, M., Blankson, A. N., Calkins, S. D., & Keane, S. P. (2009). "Family Stress and Parental Responses to Children's Negative Emotions: Tests of the Spillover, Crossover, and Compensatory Hypotheses." Journal of Family Psychology. Kwon, K. A., Han, S., Jeon, H. J., & Bingham, G. E. (2013). "Mothers' and Fathers' Parenting Challenges, Strategies, and Resources in Toddlerhood." Early Child Development and Care. S. J., Altschul, I., & Gershoff, E. T. (2013). "Does Warmth Moderate Longitudinal Associations Between Maternal Spanking and Child Aggression in Early Childhood?" Developmental Psychology.

2. **Pay attention to the present moment without judging it.**
   The goal is simple: Be aware of what's happening right
   now without criticizing it.
3. **Let judgments come and go.** When judgments arise,
   acknowledge them and let them pass.
4. **Keep bringing your focus back to the present moment.**
   Our minds often wander, so the practice is about gently
   returning to the here and now.
5. **Be gentle with yourself.** Don't judge your thoughts; just
   notice when your mind wanders and gently guide it back.[4]

A simple method that you can try anywhere is:

- Stand tall and focus on your breath. Take a few quiet
  breaths.
- Feel the ground beneath your feet, making sure they're
  firmly planted.
- Slowly shift your weight to the right while keeping both
  feet on the ground. Try to stay balanced.
- Repeat the weight shift to the left, front, and back, noticing
  how far you can lean before losing balance.
- Pay attention to how you focus on shifting your weight
  and maintaining balance throughout the exercise.

Another simple technique:

- Take a moment to calmly look around you.
- Name five things you see, four things you feel, three things
  you hear, two things you smell, and one thing you taste.
- Notice how it feels to focus on the present moment.

---

4. Mindful, "Getting Started with Mindfulness," (n.d.) https://www.mindful.org/
meditation/mindfulness-getting-started/.

- As an extra tip, you can also do this exercise with colors. Look around and focus on different colors and shades, shifting your focus from your thoughts to the world around you.

We're not trying to make these feelings go away. We're just observing them without reacting. This helps us stay in the moment and keep perspective. When we're out, commuting, or waiting at the school gates, we can bring our attention back to our body and surroundings, keeping us grounded and giving us a chance to breathe.

Here is another method that goes more deeply into attaining a state of mindfulness:

- Sit comfortably and close your eyes or relax your gaze.
- Focus on your breath. Notice how you're breathing without trying to change it.
- Shift your attention to yourself and ask, "How am I feeling today?"
- Notice any thoughts, emotions, or physical sensations without judging them.
- Ask yourself, "What do I need right now? What can I do for myself?"
- Take three deep breaths to finish the check-in.
- Slowly return to the present moment at your own pace.[5]

That's the practice. It's simple but not always easy. The key is to keep doing it, and you'll see results over time.

---

5. Lisanne Buisman, "5 Short Mindfulness Exercises and Techniques OpenUp," OpenUp, October 27, 2023 https://openup.com/self-guided-care/blog/mindfulness-exercises/.

Next, we look at meditation techniques for mindfulness.

MEDITATING ON MINDFULNESS

Once you've practiced being in the present moment, you can begin trying some meditation techniques. There are many meditation methods. Some of the most popular are:

- **Guided Meditation**: A guide helps you visualize relaxing scenes
- **Mantra Meditation**: Repeated calming words block distractions
- **Qigong**: Combines meditation, relaxation, movement, and breathing from Chinese medicine
- **Tai Chi**: Slow, gentle martial arts movements with deep breathing
- **Yoga**: Postures and breathing exercises for flexibility and calm

Don't worry about meditating the "right" way. You can go to meditation centers or group classes or meditate on your own using apps. Make meditation as formal or informal as you like. Some people meditate for an hour at the start and end of their day, but a few minutes a day is enough to make a difference.

Here are some ways to meditate on your own anytime:

- **Breathe Deeply:** Focus on your breathing, listening to and feeling each inhale and exhale through your nostrils. Breathe deeply and slowly, returning your focus to your breath when your mind wanders.
- **Scan Your Body:** Focus on each part of your body, noticing feelings like pain, tension, warmth, or relaxation.

Combine body scanning with breathing exercises; imagine breathing heat or relaxation into and out of each part of your body.

- **Repeat a Mantra**: Create your own mantra, which can be religious or not. Examples include the Jesus Prayer, the holy name of God in Judaism, or the om mantra in Hinduism, Buddhism, and other Eastern religions.
- **Walk and Meditate**: Meditate while walking by slowing your pace and focusing on each movement of your legs or feet. Think about action words like "lifting," "moving," and "placing" as you walk. Focus on the sights, sounds, and smells around you.
- **Pray**: Prayer is a common type of meditation. You can pray in your own words or use written prayers from your faith tradition. Look for examples in books or talk to your spiritual leader for resources.
- **Read and Reflect**: Read poems or sacred texts and take a moment to think about their meaning. Listen to sacred music, spoken words, or any music that relaxes or inspires you. Write your thoughts in a journal or discuss them with a friend or spiritual leader.
- **Focus on Love and Kindness**: Think of others with feelings of love, compassion, and kindness. This helps you feel more connected to others.

The more you meditate, the more it becomes part of your constant mindset. It's like taking a medicine that builds up in your body, providing immunity to the disease of anger.

Each type of meditation has features to help you meditate. These can vary based on the guide or teacher. Common features of meditation include:

- **Focused Attention**: Focusing your mind on one thing, like an object, image, mantra, or your breathing, helps clear stress and worry.
- **Relaxed Breathing**: This deep, even-paced breathing uses your diaphragm muscle to expand your lungs. This slows your breathing, takes in more oxygen, and uses your shoulder, neck, and upper chest muscles less, helping you breathe better.
- **Quiet Setting**: For beginners, meditating in a quiet place with fewer distractions like TV, computers, or phones can help. As you get better at meditation, you can do it anywhere, even in stressful places like traffic jams, work meetings, or long grocery store lines.
- **Comfortable Position**: Meditate while sitting, lying down, walking, or in other positions or activities. Stay comfortable and keep good posture for the best results.
- **Open Attitude**: Let thoughts pass through your mind without judging them.

DEEP BREATHING

Although breathing is a form of meditation, some people find just focusing on breathing alone to be more effective. Different meditation traditions use various breathing methods. In Chapter Two, I outlined a basic breathing exercise. In this section, we go more deeply into breathing.

Begin with short sessions and gradually increase the time as your nervous system adapts. Always remember to breathe with your belly. Deep breathing should make your lower abdomen move, not your upper chest or shoulders. From the different techniques in this chapter, choose what works for you.

Here are a handful of meditative breathing techniques and how they may help you promote health and relaxation in your body, no matter what's going on around you.

Diaphragm breathing

Diaphragm breathing is a fundamental breathing technique. Originating from Hindu practices, it involves slow and deep breathing. The diaphragm, situated at the bottom of the lungs, is a crucial muscle for breathing. It does about 80% of the work required for breathing, according to the American Lung Association.

Benefits: Research suggests that this technique can be beneficial for various health issues. A study published in the *International Journal of Yoga* found that it helped reduce asthma attacks and the need for medication. Another study in the *International Journal of Preventive Medicine* showed its effectiveness in reducing stress and anxiety and improving overall physical health, even among cancer patients.

How to do it: You can practice diaphragm breathing while sitting up or lying on your back.

1. Start by placing your hands on your belly, just below the navel. Inhale slowly, allowing your belly to expand like a balloon. Exhale, letting your belly sink towards your spine.
2. Next, place one hand on your ribs and the other on your belly. Inhale slowly, letting your belly soften and feeling your ribs expand.
3. Move the hand from your ribs to your upper chest, just below the collarbone. As you inhale, allow your belly, ribs, and upper chest to expand. Exhale and release tension.

4. It's recommended to practice this breathing exercise three to five times every morning, when stressed during the day, and before bedtime, for three weeks consistently. This regular practice can train your brain to respond positively to mindfulness and breath awareness.

Alternate-Nostril Breathing

Next is alternate-nostril breathing (ANYB). This is a form of controlled breathing. It's a gentle exercise suitable for those who prefer active meditation over sitting still. This technique involves breathing through one nostril at a time while manually closing the other, promoting alternate airflow and breathing.

Benefits: Research indicates that practicing ANYB can have significant health benefits. A study published in the *Journal of Education and Health Promotion* showed that participants with hypertension who practiced ANYB twice a day for five days experienced a notable reduction in both systolic and diastolic blood pressure, along with improved heart rate.

How to do it:

1. Sit comfortably and place your right hand on your knee.
2. Use your left thumb to gently close your left nostril.
3. Inhale slowly through your right nostril, then release your thumb and close your right nostril with your ring finger.
4. Hold your breath briefly, then exhale through your left nostril.
5. Inhale through your left nostril, then hold your breath and switch fingers to close the left nostril while opening the right. Exhale through your right nostril.
6. Repeat this process on each nostril 5 to 10 times.

Ocean-Sounding Breath

Known as ocean-sounding breath, this is an audible breathing technique.

1. Inhale deeply through your nose.
2. Beginners may find it easier to make the sound with their mouths slightly open while exhaling. Imagine trying to fog up a window with your breath.
3. As you advance, try exhaling without opening your mouth, maintaining the ocean sound. You can think of imitating the breathing sound of Darth Vader from *Star Wars*.
4. Repeat this process until you feel relaxed and centered.

Heart Rate Variability Biofeedback

Heart rate variability biofeedback (HRVB) is a form of biofeedback therapy training. It helps individuals synchronize their breathing with their heart rate patterns. The goal is to achieve deeper breathing, which can have positive effects on mental health. Studies have shown that HRVB may reduce symptoms of depression, stress, and anxiety, as well as improve the overall quality of life for those with chronic diseases.

1. Sit comfortably and note your current heart rate using a device like a smartwatch or app.
2. Practice deep belly breathing, imagining a roller coaster ride. Inhale deeply as if a roller coaster car is climbing up a track, and exhale as it descends. Aim for a smooth ride with slight pauses between each inhale and exhale.
3. After five breaths, check your heart rate again. The goal is to lower your heart rate below the starting number. Once

you achieve this, you can conclude your practice. If working with a biofeedback specialist, they will provide additional guidance and monitoring using specialized equipment.

MAKING HOME YOUR HAVEN

In our hectic lives, finding moments of tranquility is essential, especially within the sanctuary of our homes. Here are some tips for designing serene areas that foster relaxation for both parents and children:

- **Dedicated Relaxation Room**: Designate a specific room or corner solely for unwinding and rejuvenation.
- **Declutter**: Clearing clutter not only creates physical space but also declutters the mind, promoting a sense of calm.
- **Calming Colors**: Incorporate soothing hues like soft blues, greens, or neutrals to evoke a sense of serenity.
- **Natural Lighting**: Maximize natural light to uplift mood and create an airy ambiance.
- **Sensory Elements**: Introduce sensory elements such as soft fabrics, gentle music, or aromatic candles to engage the senses and enhance relaxation.
- **Comfortable Seating**: Choose chairs and seating options that prioritize comfort and support for extended periods of relaxation.
- **Houseplants and Flowers**: Bring nature indoors with houseplants and flowers, which not only beautify but also purify the air and promote a sense of well-being.
- **Landing Station**: Create a designated area, like a "landing station," where essentials are organized, minimizing stress and promoting a sense of orderliness.

By implementing these strategies, you can transform your home into a tranquil oasis, fostering peace and harmony for the entire family.

Incorporating mindfulness into your daily routine can significantly enhance calmness and reduce stress levels. Here's a checklist of mindfulness actions you can apply throughout the day:

- Start your morning with a five-minute meditation or mindful breathing session to set a calm tone for the day.
- Practice eating meals mindfully by focusing on the taste, texture, and aroma of your food, slowing down mealtime and appreciating the moment.
- Take short mindfulness breaks during the day, especially during transitions between activities. Focus on your breathing or observe your surroundings to center yourself.
- Practice mindful listening when interacting with others. Focus fully on the speaker and resist the urge to plan your response while they're talking.
- Integrate small moments of physical activity like stretching or walking into your day. Focus on the movement and physical sensations to stay present.
- Set random reminders throughout the day to pause and practice a quick mindfulness exercise, such as taking three deep breaths or feeling your feet on the ground.
- Reflect on three things you appreciate about your day or your family before bedtime, shifting focus from stress to gratitude.

By following this checklist, you can effectively integrate mindfulness into their daily routines, leading to a more balanced and less stressful family life. This approach not only reduces personal stress but also models positive behavior for children, fostering a harmonious family environment.

In the next chapter, we look at communication skills that will help enhance tranquility in your family.

CONSIDER YOUR OWN EXPERIENCE

By staying calm, you increase your resistance against any kind of storms. [1]

— MEHMET MURAT İLDAN

Let's pause for a moment and take a different angle on all of this. The primary reason you picked up this book was probably because you were worried about how your anger is affecting your children and your relationship with them, but let's also think about your own experience. A lot of energy goes into anger, and when it leads to conflict with your children, it becomes even more stressful. You're experiencing that stress every time your anger takes over. I think about it sometimes with my dad. Remember that story I told you about the time I cut my own hair? If he had been able to laugh it off and take me to the barber to get it fixed without allowing it to rile him, he would probably have had a far better experience himself. It might even have been fun for him. In contrast to what happened to my friend Shane when he left his school bag on the bus and his dad turned retrieving it into an adventure, I imagine his experience being far worse.

I want you to look back on your parenting experience and remember the fun, not the anger. Parenting is hard work, and it's even harder if we're angry all the time. I want you to do this for you as much as you're doing it for your children—because you all deserve a good experience. I want that for all parents, and I wish

---

1. "Best of Calmness Quotes." BetterSleep. Last modified March 9, 2021. https://www.bettersleep.com/blog/best-of-calmness-quotes

my dad could have seen the funny side of moments like that terrible hair-cutting experiment. If you crave a calmer and more joyful parenting experience, this work you're doing on yourself now will help you to achieve it, and if you, like me, would wish this for anyone, take a moment now to share this book with other parents.

By leaving a review of this book on Amazon, you'll help new readers find it easily, and you'll reassure them that they aren't the only ones struggling to manage their anger.

As you might know yourself, parents often feel guilty about experiencing these emotions, and even guiltier about how they express them, and this can make it difficult for them to admit it and get the help they need. By showing them that this is a common experience and there are resources out there that can help them, you could make all the difference in their journey towards a happier and calmer parenting experience.

Thank you so much for your support. There's no shame in feeling anger sometimes, and we can all help each other out as we strive to become better.

Scan the QR code below

5

LEVERAGE COMMUNICATION

> *We spend the first twelve months of our children's lives*
> *teaching them to walk and talk and the next twelve telling*
> *them to sit down and shut up.*
>
> — PHYLLIS DILLER (ACTRESS AND COMEDIAN)

S ix years. That's the average amount of time you have to converse with your child.

Think about it. Before they're six years old, you can't have any real conversations with them. They're too busy asking questions: "Why is the sky blue?" "Where does the sun go at night?" "How did I fit in Mommy's belly?" "Does that fat man have a fat skeleton?" and that perennial favorite, "Are we there yet?"

Then, when they're teenagers, you're the one asking the questions —"How was school?" and, in response, they grunt. By the time you can have a real conversation with them again, they're not kids anymore, and you're either a grandparent or dying.

If you want to have more quality time with your kids when they're kids, communication is key. The relationship you establish with them in those formative years will persist into their teenage period (hopefully!) and adulthood. This chapter will show you how to do this.

We look at active listening, assertive speaking, and conflict resolution. By learning these techniques, you will be able to communicate more effectively with your children. This will foster a supportive and less confrontational home environment.

This chapter explores the L component of the C.A.L.M.S. Anger Management Toolkit framework. It incorporates Strategy 6 (effective communication to express needs and boundaries clearly and respectfully) and Strategy 7 (conflict resolution skills to resolve conflicts peacefully and constructively). The guidance provided here will help you express feelings effectively and resolve conflicts without resorting to anger.

FIVE WAYS TO TALK TO YOUR CHILD SO THEY WILL LISTEN

Good communication is key to a healthy relationship, especially between you and your child. Your child wants a warm and loving bond with you, and effective communication can help achieve that. Sometimes, difficult family events like separation or divorce can make your child reluctant to open up. Here are five strategies to help you strengthen your relationship through better communication.

Understand Your Child's Communication Style

Some children are chatty, while others are more reserved. Regardless of your child's style, it's important that they feel comfortable coming to you with anything. Learning how your child likes to communicate can help you connect with them better. Even if your child doesn't like talking much, spending quiet time together can encourage them to open up when needed.

Avoid Lecturing

As a parent, you'll need to ensure your child listens to and understands you. However, lecturing and nagging are not effective ways to get through to them. If a conversation isn't going well, take a break. Reflect on what you want your child to understand and how they can best hear it next time you talk.

Be an Active Listener

Practice active listening when talking with your child. Give them your full attention to show you care about what they say. This means making eye contact and setting aside distractions like your phone. When it's your turn to speak, respond thoughtfully. Later, refer back to your conversation to show you remember what they said. Pay attention to anything your child says that might be concerning, as it can provide insights into their true feelings.

Share Positive Stories

Children love stories, especially ones about their parents. Share positive and appropriate stories with your child. Avoid sharing negative or inappropriate stories about their other parent or adults in their life. Make sure the stories you share are suitable for your child's age and maturity level to ensure they understand the message.

Make Time to Talk Every Day

Both you and your child may have busy schedules, but it's important to find time to talk every day. Use seemingly small moments, like car rides, breakfast, dinner, or bedtime, to have a conversation. Even a few minutes of daily talk can significantly improve your communication with your child.

Taking these steps to enhance how you communicate with your child can strengthen your overall relationship. As your child grows, your communication will evolve, but these skills will help maintain a healthy foundation for your relationship.[1]

TIPS FOR EFFECTIVE COMMUNICATION

- **Speak Clearly**: Use language your child understands. Be clear and specific, and avoid hurtful words. Speaking kindly sets a positive example and makes your child feel respected and loved.
- **Don't Bribe**: Instead of offering rewards for basic behaviors, set clear expectations and praise good behavior. Use calm consequences to encourage better behavior when necessary, fostering trust.
- **Explain Feelings**: Help your child learn to name their emotions. Listen empathetically and without judgment. Whether they express feelings verbally or through actions, help them put words to their emotions like happy, sad, or angry.

---

1. OurFamilyWizard, "Five Strategies to Improve Parent-Child Communication," Accessed June 17, 2024, https://www.ourfamilywizard.com/blog/five-strategies-improve-parent-child-communication.

- **Have Fun Together**: Enjoy lighthearted moments with your child to strengthen your bond. Relate to their interests, joke around, and share positive experiences. Always laugh with your child, not at them.
- **Focus on Behavior**: Criticize the behavior, not the child. Instead of saying, "I don't like that you are messy," say, "I don't like it when you leave clothes on the floor."
- **Lead by Example**: Model the behavior you want to see in your child. What they see you do is just as important as what they hear you say. Keep promises to build and maintain trust.[2]

THE PARENT TRAPS

These are some typical errors parents make.[3] By avoiding them, you are less likely to get upset or angry with your child.

The Escalation Trap

The escalation trap happens in two ways. The first is when your child escalates: If your child wants something like candy or more screen time, you say no because it's too close to dinner or they've already used up their screen time. They might start whining, begging, or throwing a tantrum. If they keep this up until you give in, they learn that being louder or more persistent gets them what they want. Next time, when they hear "no" and feel frustrated, they might use the same strategy again. The trap can also work in reverse: sometimes, children teach parents to only respond when the parent escalates. For instance, you tell your kids it's time for

---

2. UNICEF, "How to Communicate Effectively with Your Young Child," n.d., https://www.unicef.org/parenting/child-care/9-tips-for-better-communication.
3. Matthew H. Rouse, "Three Common Parenting Traps," Child Mind Institute, August 19, 2024, https://childmind.org/article/three-common-parenting-traps/.

dinner while they watch TV, and they ignore you until you raise your voice. They learn they don't need to listen until you yell.

What to do: To avoid escalation, stick to your decision calmly. If you say no, ignore behavior when your child is trying to change your mind. It's tough, but it teaches them that tantrums won't work. When they calm down and return to playing quietly or talk calmly, praise them: "I like how you calmed down" or "It's great when you speak calmly."

The "It's Just a Phase" Trap

Another trap is ignoring problematic behavior, hoping it'll go away on its own. You think, "It's just a phase," and you avoid addressing it. For example, if your toddler acts aggressively during playdates—hitting, pushing, grabbing—you might think it's normal for kids to do this.

What to do: Toddlers explore behaviors like hitting or grabbing. Respond by setting clear limits. Treat their behavior as an experiment, showing what's not okay. Praise them when they behave well to help manage these behaviors.

The "You Do This on Purpose" Trap

This trap is when you interpret your child's actions as deliberate attempts to annoy or upset you. For example, if you tell your child to stop playing and get ready to leave for Grandma's, and they continue playing, you might think they're doing it on purpose to bother you.

What to do: Avoid thinking your child is trying to manipulate you. Remember, they're still learning self-control. Try to understand why they behave this way—maybe they're struggling emotionally or lack coping skills. Stay calm and plan how to respond effectively without letting anger control your reactions. This will also help you encourage positive behaviors.

HOW TO LISTEN TO YOUR CHILD

Listening to your child is the most important skill you can develop. By listening, you can:

- Hear their disappointment when they don't make the team.
- Understand their frustration when plans don't go their way.
- Acknowledge their dissatisfaction when they feel their friends have more freedom.

You don't need to "fix" everything for your children. Simply listening can have a big impact.

Active listening is a key parenting skill. It involves truly being present, understanding, accepting, and appreciating your child's perspective. By practicing active listening, you build a caring relationship where your child feels supported and understood. This secure relationship helps them become resilient, responsible, and caring individuals who are open to your love and guidance.

When you practice active listening, avoid judging or evaluating what your child is saying. Accepting their feelings is different from agreeing with them.

For instance, if your child says, "I was the only one not invited to the party," you can accept their feelings by saying, "You are upset that you weren't included," even if you know others were also not invited. Arguing with them about the facts could lead to more conflict. Accepting their view allows them to focus on their feelings and clarify their thoughts.

Acceptance is at the heart of active listening. This isn't the time to correct, teach, solve problems, or ask many questions. Instead, let your child talk without interruptions or judgment while you listen to what they have to say.[4]

To understand active listening, consider how three different fathers could respond to their 10-year-old son who wants to discuss a situation. As you read, think about how the father and son feel and how the father's responses impact their relationship.

Scenario 1:

Son: (glumly) I don't want to go to soccer practice today. It's boring.

Father: (roughly) Of course you want to go to soccer practice today. You always enjoy playing with your team.

Son: No, I don't. Besides, we're practicing drills, and I hate that.

Father: Well, you better learn to like it and to like practice, too. You don't have a choice, you know. Everyone has to do things they don't want to do.

Son: I hate soccer, and I hate practice!

This father seemed annoyed and impatient, ignoring his son's feelings. The son felt unheard and unsupported, likely learning not to turn to his father for support.

---

4. The Center for Parenting Education, "The Skill of Active Listening," Accessed June 18, 2024, https://centerforparentingeducation.org/library-of-articles/healthy-communication/the-skill-of-listening/.

Scenario 2:

Son: (glumly) I don't want to go to soccer practice today. It's boring.

Father: (sweetly) Oh, that's terrible. Practice shouldn't be boring. You're such a talented player; you need more exciting drills to keep you interested.

Son: Well, I hate practice, and I don't want to go.

Father: I'm going to call the coach and tell him he needs to come up with better drills to keep you interested.

Son: No, Dad, don't do that! I'll be fine at practice. I'm going to finish my homework now. Please don't call the coach.

This father quickly praised his son and offered a solution, but he was unable to accept his son's unhappiness. The son didn't want his father's intervention and decided he was better off not talking to him. He likely won't turn to his father if he's unhappy in the future.

Scenario 3:

Son: (glumly) I don't want to go to soccer practice today. It's boring.

Father: (neutrally) You're not happy with practice because it's not interesting to you?

Son: Yeah. Nobody likes it. And the coach doesn't even notice when we're not paying attention.

Father: It bothers you that the other kids don't take it seriously.

Son: They make fun of me when the coach isn't looking. They kick the ball at me. I hate that. And the coach doesn't even see it. He's so clueless.

Father: You're really upset with the kids and feel let down that your coach isn't aware of what's happening. You expect him to know what's going on.

Son: Yeah. I want to let him know what the other kids are doing.

This father didn't get angry or jump in with solutions. Here's what he did to help his son handle the situation:

- He listened without judging.
- He tuned in to what his son was saying and feeling.
- He kept himself separate from the situation his son was describing.
- He was able to tolerate his son's sad, angry, and disappointed feelings.

As a result, the son could talk about the situation in more detail, and the father learned what was really bothering him. This scenario shows how active listening can help empower your child by helping them understand their feelings and decide how to handle a situation, ultimately bringing the parent and child closer together.

Here are some guidelines that you might find helpful in such situations:

- Accept the feelings and perceptions of your child.
- The feelings are real for them, even if you do not agree with your child's perception.
- Be objective and keep your feelings separate from your child's.
- Use your knowledge about your child to intuit what his feelings might be.
- Allow your child to be responsible for his own feelings.

- Stay separate from his experience.
- Take the time necessary to listen.
- When you can, stop what you are doing to give your child your full attention when he needs to talk to you.
- Recognize that feelings are often transitory.
- Often, once a child can vent his feelings, they lose their intensity, and he can move on quickly. It is said that positive feelings cannot come through until negative feelings come out. After that, your child will be more able to focus on solutions.
- Let the exchange go only as far as your child wants it to.
- Don't push him to continue to talk after he seems satisfied or wants to stop.
- Allow your child to draw his own conclusions.
- Be patient.
- Do not have some specific result in mind.

By becoming a haven for your children, they will see you as someone they can turn to in difficult situations, even during their teen years when they could face complicated life choices.

When you start using active listening, it can be tough to find the right words. Here are some rephrased sentence starters to help you respond and understand your child's feelings. Many parents keep these handy as a cheat sheet until they become more comfortable using them.

- "It sounds like you feel . . ."
- "Someone might feel that way because . . ."
- "You wish that . . ."
- "You want to change . . ."
- "The difficult part of this is . . ."
- "It upsets you that . . ."

- "You're unsure about . . ."
- "You're worried about . . ."
- "It seems unfair to you that . . ."

ASSERTIVE PARENTS ARE NOT ANGRY PARENTS

Assertive parenting blends the warmth of permissive parenting with the structure of authoritative parenting. It is not authoritarian parenting, which is strict and demanding. Instead, assertive parenting involves setting boundaries and expectations while valuing the child's opinions and feelings.

Unlike permissive parenting, which has few rules, and authoritative parenting, which might not always consider the child's viewpoint, assertive parenting combines structure with empathy. This approach helps children become disciplined, confident, self-aware, and good decision-makers.

Here are some key principles for assertive parents:

- **Communicate Clearly**:
  - Express expectations and feelings in a straightforward but respectful way.
  - Ensure children understand what is expected without feeling belittled.
- **Set Boundaries**:
  - Establish reasonable boundaries and consistently enforce them.
  - Explain the reasons behind rules so children understand and feel secure.
- **Encourage Independence**:
  - Allow children to make choices within set limits to build decision-making skills and responsibility.

- ◦ Guide rather than control, letting children learn from their experiences.
- **Be Consistent and Respectful**:
  - ◦ Be consistent so children know what to expect, which builds trust.
  - ◦ Respect the child's feelings and opinions, even if they differ from the parent's, to promote open dialogue and mutual understanding.

Balancing being an authority figure with being approachable and empathetic is crucial. You are a caring parent, not just a friend. If you have clear boundaries and mutual trust, challenging behavior is less common. Remember, it's important to criticize your child's behavior, not the child's inherent value. For example, say, "I was disappointed that you didn't help clear up after dinner," instead of, "You are lazy."[5]

THE GRUNT YEARS

In the early years, using a more authoritative approach with clear expectations and boundaries helps shape behavior and foster discipline. If your child is a teen, however, you'll need to use a more collaborative approach to maintain mutual respect and understanding.

Teenagers generally want independence and find it necessary to challenge authority. They do this by dressing like one another in brands that advertisements tell them to buy (using their parents' money). Nonetheless, opposing you as their parent convinces them that they are thinking for themselves. But your concern isn't their

5. Lucy Russell, "Assertive Parenting: The Incredible Benefits for Your Child," They Are The Future, December 7, 2023, https://www.theyarethefuture.co.uk/assertive-parent/.

opinions; it's your relationship with them. Open communication is key to building trust and understanding your teen's changing viewpoints. The following techniques are useful:

- **Engage in Open Dialogue:**
  - Listen with empathy and acknowledge their growing independence.
  - Encourage them to share their thoughts and feelings.
  - Foster mutual respect and help them internalize parental expectations rather than just comply.
- **Adapt Your Strategies:**
  - Shift from setting specific rules to establishing broader principles.
  - Allow more flexibility while maintaining accountability.
  - Focus on guiding decision-making rather than controlling behavior.
- **Regulate Yourself:**
  - Manage your emotions and reactions to maintain calm during challenging situations.
  - Effective self-control is crucial for assertive parenting and sets a positive example for your teen.
  - A calm demeanor fosters a harmonious home environment.

None of this is easy. Not only do teenagers believe they know more than their parents, but they also think their parents are stupid. It's useful to remember that you were probably the same way in your teens. You grew out of it. The best you can do is help them do the same.

THE VERY LOUD FAMILY

Ongoing anger between parents can lead to more conflict between parents and children. Economic stress and limited social support are particularly linked to increased parent-child conflict, which sometimes leads to child abuse. Communication skills do not remove these stressors. The quality of the parent-child relationship also affects conflict levels. Insecurely attached children, for example, tend to start more conflicts with their parents compared to securely attached children.

Research also shows that hiding family conflict can harm children.[6] In families where conflict is avoided, even when it's necessary, or where only parents can express opinions, children may face more bullying from peers. Parent-child relationships should find a balance—enough conflict to teach children how to manage disagreements safely and supportively, but not so much that it disrupts family life.

In parent-child relationships, parents usually have more power. Kids might find this frustrating, especially during conflicts, but it's normal and helps kids learn negotiation and setting boundaries, which are positive outcomes of conflict. However, in some families, kids gain more power during conflicts, which is called "coercive family processes." This shift can harm family dynamics and kids' emotional development, including how they handle conflicts with others.

Parent-child conflict in coercive families involves both parent and child behaving negatively, with actions escalating. It starts like any conflict: for example, a parent insists a child finish dinner before

6. M. Goodman, S.F. Waters, and R.A. Thompson, "Parent–Offspring Conflict," In *Encyclopedia of Human Behavior*, 28–33. Elsevier, 2012, https://doi.org/10.1016/B978-0-12-375000-6.00267-6.

dessert. The child then reacts by refusing (noncompliance). The parent might escalate by making the child stay at the table until they finish dinner, and the child may resist more by leaving without permission. This cycle continues until someone gives in (the parent allows dessert). If parents always give in, they reinforce the child's behavior, showing them that escalating conflict gets them what they want. When the child calms down after "winning," the parent giving in is reinforced by the child's calmness. This cycle feeds itself, leading to negative interactions becoming routine.

Interestingly, in some cases, these cycles start in infancy. Studies show demanding infants (those needing more attention and reacting strongly) with unresponsive mothers show more coercive behavior in toddler years. Other studies link parental traits like irritability to long-term coercive interactions. These findings support the idea that parent-child conflict can start early and continue as patterns.

As coercive cycles continue through early childhood, the parent's usual authority lessens, and kids "win" more conflicts. Over time, parents may avoid setting clear limits to avoid conflict, leading to unproductive parenting practices. This cycle impacts children's development: they may develop an inappropriate sense of control in relationships. This control extends beyond parent-child interactions, affecting how they interact with peers and others. Despite these negative effects, positive aspects of social development that come from resolving conflicts constructively may be delayed. Problems like a lack of empathy or negotiation skills may worsen, contributing to increased childhood aggression.

Children from coercive families may escalate to physical aggression if they lack other conflict-resolution skills. These children are more likely to bully peers and may lose conflicts despite their aggression. Aggressive behavior results from and fuels coercive family processes—aggressive children disobey parents more, persist in negative behavior during conflicts, and often start conflicts themselves. Not surprisingly, coercive family processes link to more externalizing problems and, in adolescence, to delinquency and even criminal behavior.

In the next chapter, we look at how you can tackle these issues through cognitive restructuring, emotional regulation, and positive parenting tactics.

6

MAINTAINING POSITIVITY

My sister, Lyla, who's in her 30s and a mom of two, convinced my wife and me to attend a parenting workshop.

One Saturday morning, Lyla became completely overwhelmed by the mess at home. As you know, if you're a parent, the first thing you must give up is orderliness. (The second thing is a schedule, and the third is sex that lasts longer than five minutes.)

Anyway, as Lyla told it, there were toys everywhere, dishes piled up, and laundry was never-ending. As she tried to clean, she got more and more frustrated and started snapping at her kids over every little thing. The whole house was tense, turning what should have been a fun day into a stressful one.

A few weeks earlier, Lyla had gone to a parenting workshop where she learned about something called cognitive restructuring. It's a method for turning negative thoughts into positive ones. She remembered this and thought she needed a new strategy to handle the cleaning madness. So, she decided to turn cleaning into a game. She called her kids into the living room and explained the new plan. Instead of treating cleaning like a boring chore, they would make it a series of timed challenges with rewards. They'd work together to finish each task before the timer went off and then take short breaks to play a quick video game or enjoy a treat.

At first, the kids weren't too sure about it, but the idea of turning cleaning into a game got them interested. Lyla set the timer for the first task—picking up all the toys in the living room. She put on some upbeat music, and to her surprise, the kids jumped right in. They raced against the clock, laughing and cheering each other on. When the timer beeped, the living room was spotless, and they celebrated with a quick dance party.

Next, they tackled the dishes. Lyla gave each child a specific job—one rinsed, the other loaded the dishwasher. They pretended to be a superhero team, each with their own special powers to defeat the dirty dishes. This made the task fun, and soon enough, the sink was empty.

As they moved through the cleaning tasks, Lyla noticed a big change in the atmosphere. The tension from earlier was gone, replaced with laughter and teamwork. The kids, who usually dreaded cleaning, were now excitedly helping and even suggesting ways to make it more fun. Lyla felt proud, not just because the house was getting clean, but because the family was happier and more connected. And best of all, there wasn't any angry yelling.

After a few hours, they had finished the major cleaning tasks. They sat down together for a well-deserved break, enjoying some home-made cookies. Lyla thought about the day and saw how well the new strategy had worked. By changing her approach to cleaning, she not only reduced conflicts but also created a sense of team-work and understanding among her family.

Lyla told me that this experience was a real turning point for her. She saw how cognitive restructuring could turn negative, and often explosive, situations into positive ones. What used to be a dreaded cleaning day had become a chance for bonding and making happy memories. She also spent less time on housework!

My wife and I didn't need to hear any more. We signed up for the workshop the next day.

This chapter introduces Strategy 8 (emotional regulation) and Strategy 9 (positive parenting) of the C.A.L.M.S. Anger Management Toolkit. You'll learn how to improve your social and emotional abilities by using techniques like cognitive restructuring, emotional regulation, and role-playing.

Before you can apply these therapies, however, it's useful to ask yourself this question: What's my family story?

THE NEVER-ENDING STORY

Family narratives play a crucial role in shaping our understanding of ourselves and our relationships within the family unit. These narratives are more than just stories. They are the threads that connect us to our past, define our present interactions, and influence our future outlook.[1]

One of the most powerful aspects of family narratives is their ability to provide support during difficult times. When families face upsetting events or conflicts, these narratives can offer a sense of continuity and resilience. They remind us that we are part of

---

1. Jeremy Sutton, "Family Conflict Resolution: 6 Worksheets & Scenarios (+ PDF)," PositivePsychology.com, November 22, 2021, https://positivepsychology.com/conflict-resolution-family-kids/.

something larger than ourselves and that challenges are a natural part of the family journey.

Consider the stories and keepsakes that connect you to previous generations. These are not just artifacts. They are symbols of resilience and endurance passed down through the family narrative. They remind us of where we come from and the values that have guided our family through generations.

Conflict is another lens through which family narratives are viewed. How does your family handle conflict? Is it through open dialogue, or does conflict manifest as shouting, anger, or withdrawal? These patterns often reflect deeper narrative structures within the family, shaping how individuals perceive and respond to conflict.

Roles within the family emerge from these narratives. Perhaps there's a "bossy" father figure or a "smart" daughter. These roles are not arbitrary; they are embedded in the family narrative, influencing expectations and interactions among family members.

Losses, too, play a significant role in family narratives. Whether it's the loss of a job, a home, or family members themselves, these events shape the family's collective identity and resilience. Understanding how these losses are narrated within the family can provide insight into coping mechanisms and support systems.

Religious, ethnic, or racial heritage also weaves through family narratives, grounding individuals in a broader cultural context and shaping family traditions and values. These narratives often evolve over generations, reflecting changes in social and cultural landscapes.

Socioeconomic status and education are additional threads in the tapestry of family narratives. How does your family perceive and value socioeconomic status? Has this position changed over generations? Similarly, what role do education and achievement play within your family? These narratives influence aspirations, opportunities, and the pursuit of success across generations.

In essence, family narratives are not just stories; they are mirrors reflecting the complexities of familial relationships, values, and resilience. By exploring and understanding these narratives, individuals can gain deeper insight into their family dynamics, strengthen connections, and navigate challenges with a greater sense of cohesion and understanding.

This is where cognitive restructuring, emotional regulation, and role-playing can help you, as a parent, change your family narrative so you can create your own stories for your children.

Let's start with cognitive restructuring.

HOW TO CHANGE YOUR MIND

Cognition is just a fancy word for how you see the world. As you know from *The Matrix*, reality exists within our brains, and as a parent, you are The One (at least until the children become teenagers). While an objective reality exists (probably), our responses to that reality are always subjective. Cognitive restructuring helps us deal more effectively with both objective and subjective reality.

In cognitive behavioral therapy (CBT), you work with a therapist to identify and change negative thought patterns. These therapists can be psychiatrists, psychologists, or other mental health professionals trained in CBT.[2]

---

2. Rebecca Joy Stanborough, "Cognitive Restructuring: Techniques and Examples," Healthline, February 4, 2020, https://www.healthline.com/health/cognitive-restructuring.

Sometimes, people have cognitive distortions—thought patterns that distort reality. These distortions can lead to depression, anxiety, relationship issues, and self-defeating behaviors. Common examples of cognitive distortions include:

- Black-and-white thinking
- Catastrophizing
- Overgeneralization
- Personalization

Cognitive restructuring helps you become aware of these negative thoughts as they happen. You can then practice reframing them in more accurate and helpful ways.

The idea is that by changing how you think about certain events or situations, you can change how you feel and how you respond to them.

Here is a five-step strategy for cognitive restructuring:

1. Write down the situation that is causing you distress. This could be anything from an event or argument to a troubling memory.
2. Identify the emotions connected to the situation. Focus on primary feelings such as fear, anxiety, sadness, depression, guilt, shame, and anger.
3. Recognize the thoughts underlying these emotions. Consider asking yourself:
   ◦ "What negative outcome do I fear?"
   ◦ "What is lacking in my life?"
   ◦ "What mistake have I made?"
   ◦ "What is unfair about this situation?"
4. Assess the situation and examine the accuracy of your thoughts. Think about the evidence that supports and

contradicts your thoughts.

5. Decide on the accuracy of your thoughts based on the evidence you've gathered. If the evidence does not support your thought, create a new, more accurate thought to replace the old one.

The goal of cognitive restructuring is to transform unhealthy beliefs and thought patterns to enhance mental health and overall well-being.

To improve cognitive thinking, you need to process your knowledge, thoughts, and experiences. Methods to enhance cognitive thinking include:

- Reducing stress
- Practicing breathing exercises
- Meditating
- Taking walks or spending time outdoors
- Exercising
- Getting sufficient sleep
- Thinking out loud
- Using concept mapping
- Identifying and changing negative thoughts
- Practicing mindfulness
- Journaling
- Focusing on positive aspects

REFRAME OF MIND

Reframing is the process of changing the way you think about memories, emotions, and situations to improve how you feel about them. Emotional reframing involves revisiting your memories and emotions and thinking about them differently to change their emotional impact, leading to improved mood and emotions.

Positive reframing means looking at negative memories, emotions, thoughts, or situations in a more positive way. It doesn't change the event itself but helps you see it from a better perspective.

A good example of reframing is viewing problems as challenges. Everyone encounters difficulties, and seeing them as problems can lead to negative feelings like helplessness and sadness. By reframing them as challenges, you see opportunities for improvement and feel more motivated.

Here are six steps to reframe your thinking:

1. Identify the thought or behavior pattern that needs to change.
2. Understand what the thought is trying to achieve.
3. Find alternative ways to achieve the same or a better outcome.
4. Create new thoughts and behaviors.
5. Take responsibility and think about the future.
6. Check in to examine alternatives.

Ask yourself questions, write in a journal, or think aloud to identify patterns and alternative ways to think. Compare the accuracy of your initial thoughts with the alternatives. Which one is more realistic? List your strengths, achievements, and qualities to help create a more positive perspective. Reframing your mindset can help you turn negative thoughts into positive and balanced ones.

THE MR. SPOCK CHALLENGE

Emotional regulation is all about handling your feelings in a healthy way. It starts with recognizing and accepting whatever emotions you're feeling without judging yourself. Whether it's frustration over a messy house like my sister or other feelings like anger, anxiety, impatience, or irritation, it's important to name those feelings and understand how they affect you physically, such as making your heart race or your breathing faster.[3]

Once you know what you're feeling, the next step is to calm yourself down. You can do this in different ways—take deep breaths, stretch your body, or step outside for a bit. These tricks help you cool off and see things more clearly.

When emotions run high, trying something unexpected can help ease the tension. Maybe it's putting on music and dancing around or doing something fun to lighten the mood. It's about showing that you can handle stress in a positive way without letting it get the best of you.

After the storm settles, take a moment to think about what set off your emotions. Was it stress from work, tiredness, or maybe something from your past? Understanding these triggers helps you deal with similar situations better next time.

Remember, it's okay to feel all kinds of emotions, even the not-so-good ones. Feeling upset doesn't mean you're a bad person. The key is to express those feelings in a way that doesn't hurt you or anyone else, especially your kids.

---

3. Meghna Singhal, "Importance of Managing Emotions as a Parent, Benefits of Controlling Emotions," ParentCircle, April 5, 2019, https://www.parentcircle.com/ways-to-control-emotions-for-parents/article.

By practicing emotional regulation, you will not only feel better yourself but also show your kids how to handle their feelings in a healthy way. It's an important skill for building strong relationships and keeping everyone in the family happy and connected.

Self-regulation is about taking a moment to think before reacting emotionally. Here are five use techniques to control your emotions:

1. **Mindful Awareness**: Being mindful helps us connect with our thoughts and surroundings. Simple exercises like controlling our breathing or focusing on our senses can calm us down and guide our actions.
2. **Cognitive Reappraisal**: This involves changing how we think about situations. It's part of therapies like CBT and dialectical behavior therapy (DBT), where we replace negative thoughts with more positive and realistic ones.
3. **Adaptability**: Emotional regulation helps us adapt to life's changes. When stressed, think about how you'd advise a friend in the same situation. It can give you perspective and help you respond more constructively.
4. **Self-Compassion**: Taking time for yourself each day and reminding yourself of your strengths can improve emotional regulation. This can include positive affirmations, relaxation techniques, and self-care activities.
5. **Emotional Support**: Building a strong emotional toolkit involves seeking support from within and from others. Mindful self-awareness and positive communication with friends or professionals can help manage emotions effectively.[4]

---

4. Madhuleena Roy Chowdhury. "Emotional Regulation: 6 Key Skills to Regulate Emotions." PositivePsychology.com, August 13, 2019. https://positivepsychology.com/emotion-regulation/.

These skills aren't just about controlling emotions—they're about using emotions constructively to bring out the best in ourselves, even during challenging times.

LIFE IS A STAGE

Role-playing is more than just a fun game—it's a powerful tool that therapists use to help people.[5] Here's why role-playing can make a big difference:

First, it gives therapists a chance to see how clients react and think in different situations. This helps them understand their clients better and figure out what they need.

Second, role-playing lets clients practice the new skills they're learning in therapy. It's like a practice run before they try it out in real life.

Third, therapists and clients work together to try out new ways of talking and acting. This helps clients learn how to communicate better, both with words and without. Another benefit is that role-playing helps clients handle different reactions they might get from others. This prepares them for all kinds of situations.

Role-playing also helps clients see how the skills they learn in therapy can work in real life. It shows them the value of what they're learning and helps them overcome challenges. It's also great for practicing social skills, being assertive, and improving how we talk to others. Therapists can interrupt during role-playing to challenge clients' negative thoughts and help them think more positively. Clients can even role-play situations they struggle

---

5. Jeremy Sutton, "Role Play in Therapy: 21 Scripts & Examples for Your Session," PositivePsychology.com, July 22, 2022, https://positivepsychology.com/role-play ing-scripts/.

with in their daily lives. This gives them a chance to find new ways to deal with tough situations.

Lastly, role-playing teaches clients how to stay calm and handle tough feelings like anxiety or anger. This can help with things like social anxiety, speaking in public, or dealing with stress.

Here's how it works. When therapists use role-playing, they give clients a chance to try out new ways of acting and responding. This helps clients see what works best for them. Therapists need to explain why they're doing it and set up the scenario clearly. They assess how clients communicate and behave in that moment. Then, they work together to come up with new ways of communicating and behaving.

Scripts can be helpful, too. They give clients a clear idea of what to say and do during role-play. This makes it easier for clients to focus and understand what's expected of them.

One common technique is the "empty chair" exercise. Here, clients imagine someone important to them sitting in a chair across from them. They talk to this imaginary person about their feelings and experiences as if they were really there. For example, a therapist might ask, "If your husband were here right now, how would he be sitting or standing? What would he look like?" This helps clients explore their feelings and practice how they might handle difficult situations. It gives therapists insight into what clients struggle with and helps them ask the right questions.

Overall, role-playing helps clients think about their feelings and try out new ways of coping and responding. It's a practical tool that can make therapy sessions more effective and meaningful.

The great thing about role-playing for a parent, though, is that kids love it! For them, it's a game. So, you can benefit psychologically from learning to control your anger, and the children can learn a lot about how not to stress out Daddy and Mommy. Here are some steps you can use to create your own role-playing exercise.

- **Step 1: Identify the situation.** To start the process, introduce the problem and encourage an open discussion to uncover all of the relevant issues.
- **Step 2: Add details.** Next, set up a scenario in enough detail for it to feel "real." Make sure that the kids (and your spouse) are clear about the challenge that you're trying to work through and that they know what you want to achieve by the end of the session.
- **Step 3: Assign roles.** Once you've set the scene, identify the various fictional characters involved in the scenario. Emphasize to your child or children that they should use their imagination to put themselves inside the minds of the people that they're representing.
- **Step 4: Act out the scenario.** Each person can then assume their role and act out the situation, trying different approaches where necessary for handling the same situation.
- **Step 5: Discuss what you have learned.** When you finish the role-play, talk about what you've learned so that you or the people involved can learn from the experience.[6]

A ROUTINE LIFE

It's important to reinforce all these exercises with action. One way to do this with the kids is to establish routines. Routines make your home organized and predictable. This helps kids and teens

6. MiindTools. "Role-Playing: Preparing for Difficult Conversations and Situatio." Accessed June 25, 2024. https://www.mindtools.com/acjtx9g/role-playing.

feel safe and cared for. Having a predictable family life can also help kids handle big changes like growing up, parents splitting up, illness, or moving to a new home. It also ensures there are fewer things for you to get angry about.

Routines that include fun activities or family time can make kids feel like they belong and strengthen family bonds. For instance, your routine might be reading a story every night before bed, eating meals together, or playing soccer with your child before practice each week.

Giving kids chores as part of their routine helps them learn to be responsible and manage their time. These are skills they'll use their whole lives. As kids get better at their routines, they also become more independent.

Routines also help younger kids learn healthy habits, like brushing their teeth, taking medicine on time, staying active, or washing hands after using the bathroom.

Daily routines also help set kids' body clocks. Bedtime routines, for example, help kids' bodies know when it's time to sleep. This is really helpful as kids get older and their bodies change.

Routines have lots of benefits for parents, too. When life gets busy or hard, routines can make you feel more organized and in control. This can lower your stress and worry. Most of all, routines often mean fewer arguments and decisions. For example, if Sunday is pizza night, you don't have to argue about what to make for dinner. (Not that kids ever argue against pizza, but this allows you to also have broccoli night with less fuss.)

Following a routine also frees up time for things you enjoy, like exercise or hobbies.[7] To create a routine, start by setting a regular

7. Kendra Cherry, "The Importance of Maintaining Structure and Routine

wake-up time and bedtime, meal times, and activities. This gives your day structure and makes it easier to manage tasks. While your schedule may change from day to day, having a basic routine helps you stay organized and less stressed.

Some people thrive with a detailed schedule, while others prefer a looser plan. Figure out what works best for you based on what you need to get done and what keeps you motivated. Remember, it's okay if your routine doesn't always go as planned. Be flexible, and don't add extra pressure. Adjusting to a new routine can take time, especially during stressful times.

Get everyone in the family involved, including the children. A routine that works well requires everyone's input. Talk about everything that you do daily in your family and make a list. Start with the times people wake, eat, bathe, do homework, complete house chores, sleep, etc. Organize the items on the list in order of when you do them each day. Then, assign roles to tasks. Help everyone to understand the tasks and their roles in the daily routine. Be realistic and allow each member to take up what they can manage.

Remind children of the routine as you go about everyday tasks. Try saying, "We always brush our teeth before bed" or "Reading first, then TV." You'll be amazed how many arguments such a simple practice stops.

While all these techniques described in this chapter are useful, you may find that you're not quite reaching where you want to be. That's why my wife and I decided to do the parenting workshop.

During Stressful Times," Verywell Mind, August 29, 2022, https://www.verywell mind.com/the-importance-of-keeping-a-routine-during-stressful-times-4802638.

In the final chapter, we look at how the skills you develop can be used to create strong support systems for you as a parent.

7

SEEKING SUPPORT

My sister Lyla, who I told you about in the previous chapter, used to face chaos every day as a working mom of two. Between her job and managing the never-ending energy of her toddlers, she often felt like she was barely keeping her head above water. At the parenting workshop, she opened up to one of the instructors, who suggested something that would change her life: a local parenting support group.

Lyla was skeptical at first. She wasn't sure if sitting in a circle talking about parenting would actually help. But with no other solutions and feeling desperate for any kind of relief, she decided to give it a shot. She felt extremely nervous walking into that first meeting, but what she found there surprised her. Instead of judgment or pity, she found a room full of parents who understood exactly what she was going through. They shared stories of sleepless nights, temper tantrums in supermarkets, and the constant struggle to find balance. It wasn't just about tips and tricks for handling toddlers; it was about emotional support and solidarity.

As the weeks went by, Lyla started looking forward to the meetings, as did her husband. Both of them learned practical strategies for managing their kids' behavior, and, more importantly, they gained confidence as parents. The group became Lyla's sounding board for tough decisions and her refuge on tough days. She no longer felt alone in her challenges.

Through that parenting group, Lyla found a community that lifted her up when she felt overwhelmed and unsure. It wasn't just about surviving anymore; it was about thriving as a parent and feeling empowered in her role.

Parents often think they're bad at parenting if their kid is having a tough time. This feeling of shame stops them from sharing with other parents. They might also believe everyone else has perfect relationships with their kids and always knows what to do. Parenting groups remind us that there's no such thing as a perfect parent or kid. Every parent has doubts, and everyone makes mistakes.

In this chapter, we look at building strong support systems, both within the family and externally, to enhance parenting effectiveness and resilience. This is the "S" component of the "C.A.L.M.S. Anger Management Toolkit" (Strategy 10—seeking support). Here, you will learn how to establish and utilize various support systems to better navigate parenting challenges, including therapy and co-parenting.

MISERY LOVES COMPANY (AND OTHER REASONS TO JOIN A PARENT GROUP)

- **They're a safe place to vent**. When you're feeling low, it's helpful to vent to others who have been there. They can share their own frustrations and reassure you that it's okay to feel the way you do. There is great value in being able to express thoughts and feelings without judgment in a place where members brainstorm ideas to help each other.

- **They're a place to share triumphs and disappointments.** Parents can share their children's milestones, like saying their first words or taking their first steps after years of therapy. These moments bring joy to everyone. It's also encouraging for younger parents to hear stories of older children making progress.

- **They help you appreciate your child.** My sister recalls a moment in a support group when one parent wished their child would stop talking to random kids, and another parent wished their child would start talking to others. This helped the first parent appreciate her child's behavior.

- **They're a place to form deep friendships.** When your child's differences make it hard for them to socialize, you can feel isolated, too. Parent groups can be a great place to form friendships with people who truly understand your situation.[1]

- **They make you feel less alone.** When you first notice your child isn't developing like their peers, or when you get a diagnosis, it's comforting to know there are other kids like yours—and other parents who understand what you're going through.[2]

1. Beth Arky, "How Parent Support Groups Can Help," Child Mind Institute, August 19, 2024, https://childmind.org/article/how-parent-support-groups-can-help/.
2. Newport Academy Staff, "Why Parenting Support Groups Are So Important," *Newport Academy* (blog), February 25, 2019, https://www.newportacademy.com/resources/restoring-families/parenting-support-groups/.

You don't need to join a workshop to find a parent group. You just need to connect with other parents. If you're looking to expand your parent network, here are some tips to get started:

- **Attend School Events.** You're already going to your child's school events, so why not make the most of it? Start chatting with other parents while you're there. You'll be surprised at how eager others are to connect. You already have one significant thing in common, and soon enough, you'll discover many more shared interests.
- **Schedule Playdates.** Playdates are a win-win situation—your child gets to hang out with friends, and you might make a new friend, too. As your child plays with different friends, you'll meet their parents and eventually find the ones you really click with. Not everyone will be your cup of tea, and that's perfectly fine!
- **Join a Mommy & Me Group.** When your kids are very young, joining a Mommy & Me group is an excellent way to meet other local parents early in your parenting journey. There are plenty of activities like Mommy & Me yoga or music classes where you can connect and have fun with other parents.
- **Try a Parent App.** If you're unsure where to start, there's an app for that! Apps like Peanut (often called Tinder for Moms) help parents connect virtually, making it easier to navigate the ups and downs of parenting together.
- **Connect Virtually in a Facebook Group.** There are plenty of great Facebook groups for parents to connect.[3]

---

3. Kaitlin Willow, "5 Ways to Build a Parent Network," Once Upon a Farm, April 6, 2023, https://onceuponafarmorganics.com/blogs/upon-a-blog/ways-to-build-a-parent-network.

Parents of Special Needs Children

When your child first starts having challenges—whether at birth, as a toddler, or during school years—it can be confusing and isolating. You might feel like you don't know anyone going through the same thing, and sharing your struggles with friends whose kids seem to be hitting all their milestones can be tough. Even after getting a professional diagnosis, you might have lots of questions that your clinician can't answer.

This is where special-needs communities come in. Finding other parents who are dealing with similar issues can make navigating this unexpected path a lot easier. Thanks to the internet, it's just a few clicks to find support groups both online and offline through nonprofits, Facebook pages, Meetup groups, and local listservs. Often, these connections can lead you to other groups until you find the right fit.

PARENTS VS. PARENT EXPERTS

As useful as parent groups are, sometimes they're not enough. Maybe your situation is more extreme, or maybe you (or your children) have special challenges. That's where professional therapy is useful. Admitting you need mental health support isn't easy. Some folks feel embarrassed; others can't talk to their family or friends about it, and, for many, the cost is just too high.

However, if you're worried about how to fit therapy into your budget, don't stress—there are other ways to get the help you need. There are plenty of mental health resources that are convenient and affordable.

Here are some tips on how you can get the help you need:

Check Your Insurance

If you have insurance through work, see if your plan includes essential mental health services like therapy, counseling, inpatient services, and substance use treatment.

Stick to an "in-network" therapist if you can since "out-of-network" ones might not be covered and could cost more. Not all therapists take insurance, so check before booking an appointment to see if they accept your plan. Sometimes, you might need a referral for certain services, so it's best to check with your insurance provider first.

If you don't have insurance or your therapist doesn't take it, there are still options. Many therapists offer sliding scale fees based on your income. It's worth asking, even if they don't advertise it. You can also ask about shorter sessions, which cost less, or meeting less frequently, like every other week. (However, experts usually advise against meeting less than once a week for the best results.)

Meet with a Psychologist in Training

Consider checking out a psychologist training clinic. These are often at universities and colleges where students are training to become therapists. While your therapist is in training, they'll be supervised by a licensed professional. Interns are hardworking, have the latest training, and often cost less.

Look into Community Mental Health Centers

Local community mental health centers are another great resource. They understand local issues and cultural attitudes around mental health. They also help reduce the stigma of mental illness and have been shown to help lower suicide rates.

Try Online Therapy Services

If fitting therapy into your schedule is tough, consider online therapy. It has become more available since the COVID-19 lockdowns. Online therapy can be just as effective as in-person for some people, especially if you travel a lot or have physical disabilities. You can meet your therapist over video calls or text messages. Services like Therapy Aid, Talkspace, and BetterHelp offer free or discounted trials, and many accept insurance.

Check Whether Your Employer Has an Employee Assistance Program

Some employers offer Employee Assistance Programs (EAP) that include free counseling for personal or work-related stress. These sessions are confidential but limited in number.

Look For Local And Online Support Groups

Nonprofits and local organizations offer free support groups for issues like grief, trauma, and addiction recovery.

Self-Help Books, Meditation Apps, And Podcasts

Self-led activities can boost your mental and physical health. Check your local library or discount bookstores for self-help books. There are free mental health apps for meditation, anxiety, and PTSD support and plenty of mental health podcasts. While these can't replace therapy, they can be very helpful.

Dear God

Faith-based help can offer compassion and understanding that are aligned with your values. Talk to people in your congregation or look for support groups. Social support and community connections can do wonders, even if they aren't explicitly focused on mental health.

No matter your situation, there's a way to get the help you need.[4] It's also worth noting that a meta-analysis of psychological treatments has found counselors are just as effective as psychologists, just much cheaper. The key is that the client is comfortable with the therapist and trusts them. Also, different kinds of therapy are equally effective, and the time you spend in therapy makes no difference, meaning once you feel you're done, you're done.[5] In fact, if your therapist keeps saying you need to continue, that in itself might be a red flag.

The Challenges of Co-Parenting

It's a harsh reality, but the chances of your marriage ending in divorce range from 2 in 5 to 1 in 2. The odds depend on various factors: you're more likely to get divorced if you get married in

4. Steven Rowe, "What to Do When You Can't Afford Therapy," Psych Central, December 4, 2012, https://psychcentral.com/blog/what-to-do-when-you-cant-afford-therapy.
5. Mary L. Smith, and Gene V. Glass. "Meta-Analysis of Psychotherapy Outcome Studies," American Psychologist 32, no. 9 (1977): 752–60, https://doi.org/10.1037/0003-066X.32.9.752.

your early twenties, are less educated, and are not financially stable.[6]

Having to raise your children when you're no longer together with their father or mother inevitably adds to the stress of parenting. That makes it easier to succumb to anger. If you can co-parent effectively, however, that reduces possible triggers. It can even make you less prone to get angry (if only because you no longer have to interact with your former spouse every day).

To make co-parenting successful, you must distinguish your personal relationship with your ex from your co-parenting relationship. Think of this new relationship as one solely focused on the well-being of your children. Remember, your marriage may be over, but your family is not. Acting in your kids' best interest is your top priority. The first step is to always put your children's needs ahead of your own.

Through cooperative co-parenting, your children will realize they are more important than the conflict that ended your marriage. This understanding can help them thrive despite the changes. Kids whose divorced parents have a cooperative relationship:

- **Feel Secure**: Confidence in the love of both parents helps kids adjust more quickly and easily to divorce and new living situations, enhancing their self-esteem.
- **Benefit From Consistency**: Co-parenting fosters similar rules, discipline, and rewards between households, so children know what to expect and what's expected of them.

---

6. "FastStats," March 13, 2024, https://www.cdc.gov/nchs/fastats/marriage-divorce.htm.

- **Better Understand Problem-Solving**: Observing parents work together teaches children how to effectively and peacefully solve problems.
- **Have a Healthy Example to Follow**: Cooperative parents set a life pattern children can carry into the future, helping them build and maintain strong relationships.

Here are seven tips to help you co-parent effectively:

1. **Set hurt and anger aside.** Successful co-parenting requires you to put your own emotions—anger, resentment, or hurt—on the back burner in favor of your children's needs. This may be the hardest part of co-parenting, but it's essential. Co-parenting is about your child's happiness, stability, and future well-being, not about your feelings or those of your ex-spouse.
2. **Separate feelings from behavior.** It's okay to feel hurt and angry, but your feelings shouldn't dictate your behavior. Let your child's best interests—working cooperatively with the other parent—motivate your actions.
3. **Let your feelings out somewhere else.** Vent to friends, therapists, or even a pet, but never to your child. Exercise can also provide a healthy outlet for letting off steam.
4. **Stay kid-focused.** When feeling angry or resentful, remember that your child's best interests are at stake. Looking at a photo of your child can help you calm down.
5. **Don't put your children in the middle.** While you may never completely lose your resentment or bitterness about your breakup, compartmentalize these feelings. Keep your issues with your ex away from your children.
6. **Never use kids as messengers.** Using children to convey messages to your co-parent places them in the center of your conflict. Call or email your ex directly instead.

7. **Keep your issues to yourself**. Avoid saying negative things about your ex to your children or making them feel they have to choose sides. Your child has a right to a relationship with their other parent free of your influence.[7]

Some other useful strategies are:

- **Think of your ex as a business partner**. Approach your co-parenting relationship professionally, focusing on your children's best interests.
- **Find the best method of communicating with your ex**. Identify a communication strategy that works for both of you, whether it's face-to-face, through emails, or using a co-parenting app.
- **Be committed to your kids and communicate regularly with them**. Ensure your children feel supported and informed about co-parenting decisions.
- **Do not talk negatively about your ex in front of your children**. Maintain a positive environment for your children by avoiding negative remarks about their other parent.
- **Use the "I" message**. Express your feelings and needs without blaming your co-parent. For example, "I feel concerned when . . ."
- **Control your impulses**. Avoid reacting impulsively during disagreements. Take a moment to calm down before responding.

---

7. Jocelyn Block and Melinda Smith, "Co-Parenting and Joint Custody Tips for Divorced Parents," November 2, 2018, https://www.helpguide.org/family/parent ing/co-parenting-tips-for-divorced-parents.

- **Use the "10-Second Rule."** Pause for 10 seconds before responding to potentially inflammatory statements to avoid escalating conflicts.
- **Actually listen**. Make a genuine effort to understand your co-parent's perspective during discussions.
- **Be sure to stay on topic**. Keep conversations focused on the children and avoid bringing up past issues or unrelated topics.
- **Be willing to compromise**. Show flexibility and a willingness to find a middle ground for the sake of your children.

5 KEYS TO CO-PARENTING COMMUNICATION

Effective co-parenting rests on effective communication. Use these strategies to avoid misunderstandings, disagreements, and arguments:

1. **Practice Effective Communication Skills**. Start a conversation with your co-parent and share your concerns from your point of view. Be open to different perspectives and finding a compromise. A solution both of you can agree on, even if it's not perfect, is better than a great solution that only one of you likes.

2. **Control your emotions**. It's normal to feel strong emotions when discussing issues about your children, especially if there are unresolved feelings from the separation. Recognize when you're getting angry, and find ways to manage it, like taking deep breaths or stepping away for a bit. If things get too heated, politely end the conversation by saying something like, "This isn't working. I'm hanging up now." Be willing to continue the discussion later, maybe in a neutral place.

3. **Schedule Regular Co-Parenting Calls**. Plan a regular call with your co-parent to talk about parenting issues. Stick to an agenda and have all the necessary information, like calendars, handy. Start the call by checking if it's still a good time to talk and share something positive about the kids to set a good tone.

4. **Treat Your Co-Parent with Respect**. Involve your co-parent in decisions about the children. Speak positively about your co-parent to the kids and respect their time and parenting style, even if you don't always agree. Say thank you when they treat you well and apologize when you make mistakes.

5. **Maintain boundaries**. Set boundaries to help manage your reactions to things that don't support your co-parenting goals. Avoid engaging in blaming, insulting, or unproductive communication. Remember, there will be many things you can't control at the other parent's house, so don't try to micromanage them.[8]

In the next chapter, we delve into advanced emotional management techniques and expand cultural insights. We will explore strategies and resources to enhance parenting skills. If enough parents learn them, they can have a lasting impact on future generations.

---

8. David C. Webb, "Five Ways to Improve Your Coparenting Communication," KidsFirst, n.d., https://www.kidsfirstcenter.org/siteglide-blog/five-ways-to-improve-your-coparenting-communication.

8

CONTINUING YOUR GROWTH

I f you and your spouse have different ideas about raising children, that can cause added stress to parenting. However, until I met Ming-Na and Clark (not their real names) at our parenting workshop, it never occurred to me that entire cultures had different concepts about what was best for children.

As Ming-Na and Clark revealed at one of the workshop sessions, they had always known their different upbringings would influence their parenting. But it wasn't until their three children —Phillip, May, and Nicholas—came along that the cultural contrasts became strikingly (and irritatingly, according to Ming-Na) clear.

Ming-Na, a Chinese American woman in her 30s, grew up in a household where discipline and respect for elders were paramount. Clark, a white liberal American, had parents who valued autonomy and self-expression. This difference was first noticeable at meal times. Ming insisted on family meals, complete with the expectation that the children would eat everything on their plates without fussing. Clark, on the other hand, believed in giving the kids choices, allowing them to decide what they wanted to eat (which resulted in mac and cheese for lunch, dinner, and sometimes breakfast).

When it came to education, Ming was all about rigorous academics and extracurriculars. She enrolled the kids in math camps and piano lessons, emphasizing the importance of hard work and perseverance. Clark was fine with this, but he believed in a more balanced approach. He encouraged the kids to explore their interests, even if it meant spending more time on art or sports instead of academics.

Discipline was another battleground. Ming believed in firm boundaries and clear consequences. She was quick to correct any misbehavior with a stern talk or a timeout. Clark preferred a more lenient approach, using reasoning and discussions to help the kids understand their mistakes. This often led to arguments between the two, as Clark felt Ming was too strict, while Ming thought Clark was too soft.

The couple soon realized that they either had to find common ground or a murder weapon that would leave no traces. So, they began having weekly family meetings where they discussed their concerns and parenting strategies. Ming agreed to incorporate more of Clark's flexible meal options, introducing the kids to a mix of traditional and new foods. Clark, in turn, supported Ming's structured approach to education but found ways to make learning fun and engaging.

For discipline, they adopted a hybrid approach. They established clear rules and consequences but also incorporated Clark's method of discussing feelings and reasoning through problems. This combination allowed them to maintain order while fostering an environment of understanding and empathy.

Through compromise and open communication, Ming and Clark managed to blend their diverse parenting styles. They created a family dynamic that honored both their cultural backgrounds, ultimately raising their children in a loving, balanced, and respectful environment.

WHY PARENTS ARE LIKE FISH

Most of us assume that the parenting practices we see in our society are standard everywhere. We might disagree with individual parents' approaches, but there are always some "basics" that we believe are universal. However, culture is like the water a fish swims in—the fish is not aware it is in a fishbowl or a river or the sea.

I think it's important for all parents to understand this and not just those who are in multicultural relationships. A lot of the stress in parenting comes from believing there's a right way and a wrong way to do things. When we see that a particular approach doesn't work, we tend to blame ourselves, sometimes our spouse, and maybe even our children. However, once we realize that parenting in our society is just one flavor of raising children, that knowledge helps us cope. We are less likely to get triggered, and we worry less that we're getting it wrong.

As one anthropologist notes: "The parental practices we follow in the West are merely cultural constructions that have little to do with what is 'natural' for babies ... In America, social independence is favored, so babies are regulated and encouraged toward independence ... every culture is self-righteous about its parenting style and goals and disapproving of the parenting style of others."[1]

---

1. Meredith F. Small, *Our Babies, Ourselves: How Biology and Culture Shape the Way We Parent*, Anchor Books, 1998.

So, parenting styles can be wildly different depending on where you are in the world. Culture shapes the way we raise our kids.

In places like China, parenting is all about group harmony and the greater good of the community. There, the needs of the family and community often come before individual desires. It's all about interdependence and making sure everyone thrives together. This approach builds strong family bonds and a deep sense of belonging.

In the United States, especially among white Americans, parenting often emphasizes independence and self-expression. Kids are encouraged to pursue their interests, make their own decisions, and express their individuality. This can foster creativity and self-confidence but sometimes makes setting boundaries a bit tricky.

In many African cultures, authoritative parenting is common, emphasizing respect for authority and rule-following. This can promote discipline but might stifle creativity. On the flip side, more permissive parenting styles are seen in other parts of the world, where independence and self-expression are highly valued, boosting creativity but sometimes leading to challenges in setting boundaries.

Here are some more parenting practices in different countries, some of which you will almost certainly consider wrong.

- **Norway and Scandinavia**: Even in the harshest winters, babies in Norway and other Scandinavian countries are bundled up warmly and nap outside in strollers. Fresh air is highly valued. In Denmark, parents often leave their strollers with babies on the sidewalk while dining at a restaurant.
- **Italy**: Children in Italy are commonly allowed to sip alcohol or wine with family during meals. Although most

European countries have an 18-year-old drinking limit, supervised drinking within the family is generally accepted. This custom is evolving but is still seen in practice.

- **France**: French schools allocate at least 30 minutes for lunchtime. Lunchtime is a social affair and an opportunity to try new foods. French parents emphasize slowing down and savoring meals.
- **Japan**: Japanese children learn responsibility and self-control early on. They participate in "cleaning time" at school and home, maintaining a tidy environment. Young children often use public transport independently. Parents prioritize giving children the tools to explore the world on their own. [2]
- In the Caribbean, raising a child is often seen as a community effort. Extended family members and neighbors play an active role in a child's upbringing. This communal approach provides a strong support system and ensures that children are well cared for and connected to their cultural roots.
- In India, parenting often blends modern approaches with traditional values. Family is paramount, and respect for elders is emphasized. Parents are highly involved in their children's education and moral development, ensuring that cultural traditions are passed down through generations.
- In some South American hunter-gatherer communities, parenting is very hands-on and community-based. Kids are carried most of the day, breastfed on demand, and sleep with their parents. There's a lot of freedom for

---

2. Psychologs Magazine. "Understanding Cultural Differences in Parenting Practices," June 17, 2023. https://www.psychologs.com/understanding-cultural-differences-in-parenting-practices/.

children to explore and play, which is considered crucial for their development.

PARENTING PSYCHOLOGIES

Our culture dictates what kind of approach is permissible at the family level. In the West, psychologists put parenting styles into four categories: authoritarian, authoritative, permissive, and neglectful.

Authoritarian parents run a tight ship, being strict and bossy. Kids with these parents often have a harder time managing themselves and their feelings. Authoritative parenting strikes a balance, being warm and caring while also setting clear rules that make sense for the child's age. These parents prefer guiding their kids with reasoning over punishments, and they make sure their children feel heard in family decisions. This style is usually linked with great outcomes for the kids.

On the flip side, permissive parents are all about love and putting their kids first, but they don't really set boundaries. This can lead to kids developing behavioral issues and bad habits. Lastly, uninvolved or neglectful parents don't show much affection or set any limits. Their kids often end up with the worst results compared to other parenting styles.

Stop a bit and think about which style you use. If it's authoritarian, you're more likely to get triggered and angry when your kids don't do what you want. So, you may want to work on that because it may harm your relationship with them.

Bear in mind that these findings mostly apply to developed Western societies. Studies of other countries have been mixed. For example, authoritarian parenting is more common in Asian and African cultures, where parents emphasize respect for authority, rule-following, and conformity. In South Korea and Singapore, over 90 percent of adults believe spanking is necessary for discipline. In South Africa, the number is 82 percent.[3] Yet, although spanking is correlated to lower academic achievement and higher delinquency among children in Western nations, East Asian children do better on a host of outcomes, particularly academics, compared to African children.

The same is true for Korean-American families. Research shows that over 75% of these families don't fit neatly into the standard parenting categories. Traditional Chinese child-rearing, similarly, doesn't have a direct equivalent to the Western concept of authoritarian parenting. Still, if you're a Western parent living in a Western country, spanking is not a good idea. It's bad for you since resorting to physical punishment may make your anger worse, and it's certainly bad for your long-term relationship with your kids.

Looking at hunter-gatherer societies, you'll find parents who almost never get angry with their children. Kids are given a lot of freedom to explore, even in situations that might seem neglectful by Western standards. If a baby grabs a dangerous tool, no one rushes to take it away. When kids act out aggressively, parents might ignore it, laugh, or simply separate the kids instead of disciplining them. Physical punishment is rare, and while this might not fit the authoritarian or authoritative molds, it's not exactly permissive either. Instead, hunter-gatherer parents guide their children through play and social interaction, teaching them to share and overcome selfish impulses. As kids grow, they are held accountable by their community, learning from natural consequences like getting hit back if they hit someone older.

3. Murray A Straus, Emily M. Douglas, and Rose Anne Medeiros, *The Primordial Violence: Spanking Children, Psychological Development, Violence, and Crime*, New York: Routledge, 2014.

Psychological control methods like teasing or scaring children with stories about supernatural consequences are also common.

Interestingly, in some cultures, such psychological control doesn't have the same negative impact it might have in others. For instance, in a study of 12 different cultures, it was found that the connection between psychological control and internalizing symptoms was weaker in places where such control was more common.

Autonomy and freedom of choice, often seen as key components of authoritative parenting, are valued differently depending on the culture. In societies that prioritize interdependence and respect for elders, children might expect their parents to make decisions for them, viewing it as a sign of care and responsibility. In these settings, the emphasis on free choice might not be as beneficial.

Despite these cultural variations, authoritative parenting tends to be linked with positive outcomes worldwide, especially in societies where formal education is essential for success. An international meta-analysis of 428 studies found that authoritative parenting is associated with at least one positive outcome in every region, while authoritarian parenting often correlates with negative child outcomes.

So, while culture can shape the relationship between parenting style and child outcomes, authoritative parenting still frequently emerges as a beneficial approach, particularly in societies that emphasize formal education and individual achievement.[4,5]

Even within the same society, however, parenting practices are influenced by socioeconomic status, education, and personal beliefs. Although individual parents have a limited impact on their children's norms, as explained in Chapter One, parenting culture significantly shapes who you become as an adult.

So, the bottom line is that no single way of parenting is the "right" way. Each culture has its own methods, shaped by unique values and traditions. What's important is that these diverse practices all aim to raise happy, healthy children who are well-adapted to their society's norms.

---

4. Gwen Dewar, "Parenting Styles: An Evidence-Based, Cross-Cultural Guide," PARENTING SCIENCE, April 19, 2024, https://parentingscience.com/parent ing-styles/.

5. Lisa Leurs, "Achieving Parenting Harmony: Embracing Diversity in Parenting Styles," WA Centre for Perinatal Mental Health & Parenting Support, October 24, 2023, https://wacpps.org.au/achieving-parenting-harmony-embracing-diversity-in-parenting-styles/.

9

C.A.L.M.S. MASTERY—PRACTICAL STRATEGIES FOR EVERYDAY PARENTING SUCCESS

B ecoming a dad has changed me in ways I never expected. The first change that surprised me was how important that little scrap of wailing human became to me as soon as she entered the world. Instantly, I had a new purpose in life, which eclipsed all others.

The second thing that surprised me was that I could no longer talk to my childless friends—at least not in the same way. I realized that my new favorite topic, my daughter, would bore them. More importantly, I realized that I had a new perspective on life that they simply didn't share.

All this meant that, in important ways, I became a different person. Raising my two children has fundamentally changed me. There's the "me" before kids and the "me" after kids. My children push my buttons and test limits I didn't know I had. But hidden within the joys and trials of parenting is a silver lining: personal growth. Raising my son and daughter has helped me confront my limitations and unhealed wounds, offering me a chance to grow beyond what I thought possible. Here are five ways I think I've grown because of my children:

1. **Patience**: Patience isn't something I was born with, but I've learned to develop it. Children don't respond well to knee-jerk reactions or anger, and it's not good for anyone's mental health. By taking a deep breath when a favorite item gets broken or calmly talking through a toddler tantrum, I've learned to respond with more compassion and care. My kids are learning, and so am I.

2. **Presence**: Watching my kids play, I've noticed they're completely engaged and present in the moment. They don't need to meditate to find that sweet spot—they just live it. My children are masters of presence, reminding me that I can be present, too, simply by playing. I've learned to step back from the constant need to be busy or to judge and just be present by observing and witnessing.

3. **Pushing Past Comfort Zones**: As a parent, I often tell my kids to be careful, but I also need to encourage them (and myself) to push past boundaries. "Go ahead, jump in the pool—I'm right here!" My children take cues from me when it comes to courage. How I encourage or discourage them from stepping outside their comfort zone reflects my willingness to do the same.

4. **How to Fall Gracefully**: Parenting is about balancing letting go and being supportive. When my child falls, they look to me for a reaction. My response shapes theirs. My job isn't to prevent falls but to help my children see potential dangers and navigate them. Falling is a natural part of life and growth. My kids remind me that it's okay to fall—I just get back up and keep going.

5. **Gratitude**: My kids can complain despite having everything they want. I think to myself, "What do you have

to complain about?" But how often do I ask myself the same question? The universe gives me many reasons to be grateful, but I tend to focus on what's lacking. When I'm more grateful, my kids might follow suit.

This chapter summarizes practical methods for implementing C.A.L.M.S. strategies into your daily routine and maintaining these practices for long-term adaptability. The primary aim is to provide actionable guidance on integrating C.A.L.M.S. principles into everyday life, equipping you with effective tools to manage stress and promote family harmony.

SAMPLE C.A.L.M.S. PLAN: DAILY IMPLEMENTATION

C—Comprehend Your Triggers

Understanding your triggers is crucial for improving your emotional responses and overall well-being. By recognizing what sets you off, you can better navigate stressful situations and enhance your relationships. Here's how you can start comprehending your triggers and managing them more effectively.

Objective: Understand personal and family triggers

The first step in managing your emotional responses is to understand what triggers you and your family members. Triggers are specific situations, people, or events that elicit strong emotional reactions, such as stress or anger. By identifying these triggers, you can develop strategies to handle them more constructively.

Action Steps

Keep a daily log of triggers. Start by keeping a daily log of moments that trigger stress or anger. This log can be a simple notebook or a digital document where you note down the details of each incident and include the following information:

- **What happened?** Describe the situation that triggered your emotional response.
- **What were your thoughts?** Note the thoughts that crossed your mind during the incident.
- **How did you feel?** Write down the emotions you experienced.
- **What was your?** Describe how you responded to the trigger.

By regularly reviewing this log, you'll begin to notice patterns and common themes in your triggers. This insight is the first step toward understanding and managing your reactions.

Conduct weekly family discussions. Improving emotional responses isn't just an individual effort; it involves your family, too. Schedule weekly family discussions to share your triggers and explore effective coping strategies together. Here's how you can structure these discussions:

- **Share openly**. Create a safe space where everyone feels comfortable sharing their triggers without judgment.
- **Discuss coping strategies**. Talk about what has worked for each person in managing their triggers. Share ideas and suggestions.
- **Plan together**. Develop a family plan to support each other in handling triggers. This could include reminders, encouragement, or specific actions to take during stressful situations.

Regular family discussions can strengthen your bond and create a supportive environment where everyone works together to improve emotional well-being.

Engage in role-playing exercises. Role-playing exercises are a great way to practice responding to triggers constructively. Here's how you can do it:

- **Identify scenarios.** Choose common triggering situations from your daily log or family discussions.
- **Assign roles.** Have family members play different roles in the scenario. For example, one person can be the trigger, and another can be the person experiencing the trigger.
- **Practice responses.** Act out the scenario, focusing on constructive responses. This might include taking deep breaths, using calming phrases, or stepping away from the situation.
- **Take time for feedback and reflection.** After each role-play, discuss what went well and what could be improved. Offer feedback and suggestions to each other.

Role-playing helps you rehearse positive responses in a controlled environment, making it easier to apply these strategies in real-life situations.

Understanding and managing your triggers is a continuous process that requires effort and commitment. By keeping a daily log, conducting weekly family discussions, and engaging in role-playing exercises, you can develop a deeper understanding of your triggers and improve your emotional responses. This not only enhances your well-being but also strengthens your family relationships. So, start today and take the first step towards a more emotionally balanced life!

A—Always Stay Calm

Parenting can be one of the most rewarding experiences, but it also comes with its fair share of challenges. Staying calm during high-stress moments is crucial for effective parenting and maintaining a peaceful household. Here's how you can master techniques to keep your cool and create a more harmonious environment for your family.

Objective: Master techniques to maintain calm in challenging parenting situations

Staying calm isn't just about keeping your cool; it's about setting an example for your children and teaching them how to handle stress. When you can remain composed during tough times, you create a stable environment that helps your kids feel secure and learn constructive ways to manage their emotions.

Action Steps

Implement deep breathing and mindfulness exercises. One of the most effective ways to stay calm in high-stress situations is to practice deep breathing and mindfulness exercises. These techniques can help you manage your stress response and regain control over your emotions. Here's how you can incorporate them into your daily routine:

- **Deep Breathing**: When you feel overwhelmed, take a moment to focus on your breath. Inhale slowly and deeply through your nose, hold for a few seconds, and then exhale slowly through your mouth. Repeat this process several times until you feel calmer.
- **Mindfulness Exercises**: Mindfulness involves paying full attention to the present moment. When you're in a stressful situation, try to ground yourself by focusing

on your senses. Notice what you can see, hear, smell, touch, and taste. This practice can help you stay centered and prevent your mind from spiraling into anxiety.

By making deep breathing and mindfulness exercises a habit, you'll be better equipped to handle stressful parenting moments with grace.

Establish calm zones in the home. Creating designated calm zones in your home can provide a safe space for family members to regain their composure when emotions run high. Here's how to set up these areas:

- Find a quiet, comfortable area in your home where family members can go to relax and unwind. This could be a cozy corner of a room, a small nook, or even a designated spot in the garden.
- Equip the calm zone with items that promote relaxation, such as soft cushions, blankets, calming music, books, and sensory toys. You might also include stress-relief tools like stress balls or fidget spinners.
- Encourage its use. Make it a family rule that anyone can use the calm zone whenever they need a break to cool down. Encourage your kids to go there if they're feeling upset, angry, or overwhelmed.

Having a calm zone provides a physical reminder of the importance of taking a break and can help diffuse tense situations before they escalate.

Practice calm responses with children. Everyday interactions with your children are opportunities to practice and model calm responses. By doing so, you not only manage your stress better but also teach your kids valuable emotional regulation skills. Here's how to make calm responses a part of your daily routine:

- **Use a calm tone.** When addressing your children, especially during conflicts or stressful moments, speak in a calm and steady tone. This helps prevent the situation from escalating and reassures your kids that everything is under control.
- **Stay positive.** Focus on positive language and constructive feedback. Instead of saying, "Stop yelling," try, "Let's use our indoor voices."
- **Be patient.** Take a moment to listen to your child's perspective and respond thoughtfully. Show empathy and understanding, even if you need to correct their behavior.

These daily practices can turn challenging moments into teachable ones, helping your children learn to handle stress and conflict more effectively.

Staying calm in challenging parenting situations is a skill that can be developed with practice and patience. By implementing deep breathing and mindfulness exercises, establishing calm zones in your home, and practicing calm responses with your children, you can create a more peaceful and supportive family environment. Remember, your calmness is not just about managing your stress —it's about setting an example and teaching your kids how to navigate their own emotions. So, take a deep breath and embrace these techniques to bring more calm into your parenting journey.

L—Leverage Communication

Good communication is the backbone of a happy family. It builds trust, fosters understanding, and keeps everyone on the same page.

By improving how you talk and listen to each other, you can create a loving environment where everyone feels heard and valued. Here's how you can enhance family communication with clear and empathetic dialogue.

Objective

The aim is to create a space where everyone feels comfortable sharing their thoughts and feelings. It's about talking openly and listening with empathy. When you do this, you strengthen your family bonds and ensure everyone feels respected.

Action Steps

Do daily check-ins to encourage open conversations. Daily check-ins are a simple yet effective way to keep the lines of communication open. It's a regular chance for everyone to share what's going on in their lives. Here's how to get started:

- **Pick a regular time**. Find a time that works for everyone, like during dinner or before bed, when you can gather without distractions.
- **Encourage sharing**. Ask everyone to talk about their day. Questions like, "What was the best part of your day?" or "Did anything bother you today?" can get the conversation flowing.
- **Be supportive**. Listen without interrupting or judging. Offer encouragement and show you care about what they're saying.

Making daily check-ins a habit helps everyone feel more connected and understood.

Practice active listening during family meetings. Active listening is key to good communication. It means really paying attention to what someone is saying and showing that you understand. Here's how to practice it:

- **Make eye contact**. Look at the person who is speaking to show you're engaged.
- **Don't interrupt**. Let them finish their thoughts before you respond. Interrupting can make them feel like you don't value what they're saying.
- **Reflect and clarify**. Repeat what you heard to make sure you understood correctly. For example, "So, you felt left out during the group project?" This shows you're listening and helps clear up any misunderstandings.
- **Show empathy**. Acknowledge their feelings. Say things like, "I get why you feel that way," or "That sounds tough." This makes them feel validated and supported.

Active listening makes family meetings more effective and ensures everyone feels heard.

Set up a family communication board. A family communication board is a great way to keep everyone informed and connected. It's a central place for notes, reminders, and positive messages. Here's how to set one up:

- **Pick a visible spot**. Put the board in a common area like the kitchen or living room where everyone can see it.
- **Organize sections**. Divide the board into sections for different types of messages, like schedules, reminders, and positive notes. This keeps things organized.
- **Encourage participation**. Get everyone to contribute. They can leave notes about their plans, reminders for upcoming events, or positive messages for each other.

- **Keep it updated**. Regularly update the board to keep the information relevant. Remove old notes and add new ones as needed.

A family communication board helps everyone stay on the same page and promotes a sense of unity.

Improving family communication can make a huge difference in your relationships. By doing daily check-ins, practicing active listening, and setting up a family communication board, you can create a more open and supportive environment. These simple steps will help everyone feel more connected and valued. So, start today and watch your family communication thrive!

M —Maintaining Positivity

Creating a positive home environment is essential for emotional growth and overall happiness. When your home is filled with positivity, everyone feels more supported, loved, and motivated.

Objective

The aim is to build a home where positivity thrives, helping everyone grow emotionally. By focusing on the good and encouraging each other, you create a space where everyone can flourish.

Actions Steps

Start each day with a positive affirmation or motivational quote. Starting the day on a positive note can set the tone for the rest of the day. Here's how to make this a daily habit:

- **Choose a time**. Pick a time when everyone is together, like during breakfast or before heading out for the day.

- **Share positivity.** Take turns sharing a positive affirmation or motivational quote. It could be something like, "Today is going to be a great day!" or "You are capable of amazing things!"
- **Encourage participation.** Get everyone involved. Encourage each family member to come up with their own affirmations or quotes to share.

Starting the day with positivity helps everyone begin their day feeling uplifted and ready to take on whatever comes their way.

Celebrate small victories and good behavior with a family rewards system. Celebrating small victories and recognizing good behavior can boost morale and reinforce positive actions. Here's how to set up a family rewards system:

- **Identify goals.** Decide on the behaviors or achievements you want to celebrate, like completing chores, doing well in school, or showing kindness.
- **Create a system.** Set up a simple rewards system. You could use a chart with stickers or a jar where you add a token for each achievement.
- **Decide on rewards.** Choose rewards that everyone will enjoy. They don't have to be big—things like a family movie night, a special treat, or an extra half-hour of screen time can work well.
- **Celebrate together.** When someone earns a reward, celebrate as a family. Make a big deal out of it to show how proud you are of their achievements.

This system not only motivates everyone to do their best but also brings the family closer together through shared celebrations.

Promote a gratitude practice. Gratitude is a powerful tool for maintaining positivity. Sharing what you're thankful for can help everyone focus on the good things in their lives. Here's how to start a gratitude practice:

- **Encourage reflection.** Help everyone think about their day and find the positive moments. This practice helps shift the focus from what went wrong to what went right.

Practicing gratitude regularly helps everyone develop a positive mindset and appreciate the good things in life.

Maintaining positivity in your home can have a huge impact on your family's emotional growth and happiness. By starting each day with a positive affirmation, celebrating small victories with a rewards system, and promoting a gratitude practice, you can create a nurturing and uplifting environment. These simple steps can make a big difference in how everyone feels and interacts. So, start today and watch your family thrive in a positive, happy home!

S—Seeking Support

Parenting is a tough job, and no one should have to do it alone. Building and using support networks can make a huge difference in managing the challenges that come with raising a family. Here's how you can seek support and create a solid network for parenting.

Objective

The goal is to create a reliable support system both within and outside your family. This helps ensure that everyone has the resources and assistance they need to navigate parenting challenges effectively.

Action Steps

Create a family support plan. Having a clear plan can make it easier to know where to turn when you need help. Here's how to set up a family support plan:

- **Identify needs.** Think about the different scenarios where you might need support, like handling a sick child, managing school issues, or dealing with emotional stress.
- **List resources.** Write down the people and resources you can turn to for each type of support. This could include family members, friends, neighbors, or professionals like doctors and counselors.
- **Share the plan.** Make sure everyone in the family knows about the support plan and feels comfortable using it. Keep the plan somewhere accessible, like on the fridge or a family bulletin board.

Having a support plan in place can provide peace of mind and ensure you're prepared for any situation.

Join parenting groups or workshops. Connecting with other parents can be incredibly valuable. You can learn new strategies, share experiences, and feel less isolated. Here's how to get involved:

- **Find groups.** Look for local parenting groups, online forums, or social media communities where you can connect with other parents. Libraries, community centers, and schools often have information about local groups.

- **Attend workshops**. Sign up for parenting workshops or classes that cover topics you're interested in. These can provide practical advice and new perspectives.
- **Participate actively**. Engage in discussions, ask questions, and share your own experiences. The more you participate, the more you'll get out of it.

Being part of a parenting community can provide valuable support and insights that make your parenting journey easier and more enjoyable.

Encourage family members to seek individual support. Sometimes, individual support can be just as important as family support. Encourage everyone in the family to seek help when they need it. Here's how:

- **Promote counseling**. Let your family know that it's okay to seek counseling or therapy. It can be a great way to work through personal issues and gain emotional support.
- **Find mentors**. Encourage your kids to find mentors, whether it's a teacher, coach, or family friend. Having a trusted adult to talk to can be incredibly beneficial.
- **Be supportive**. Make sure everyone knows that seeking help is a sign of strength, not weakness. Offer your support and understanding if someone decides to seek individual help.

By promoting individual support, you can help each family member build resilience and emotional strength.

By incorporating the daily practices of comprehending your triggers, always staying calm, leveraging communication, maintaining positivity, and seeking support, your family can cultivate deeper connections, reduce conflicts, and foster a supportive and harmonious home environment.

The strategies you've learned will have a lasting impact on your parenting skills and family relationships.

YOUR CHANCE TO INSPIRE

The very fact that you're taking this journey and actively seeking a more positive experience for both you and your children is something to be proud of. Take a moment now to inspire someone else to start out on this path.

Simply by sharing your honest opinion of this book and a little about your own experience, you'll show other parents where they can find this guidance, and inspire them with your own story.

MAKE A LASTING IMPRESSION!

Thank you so much for your support. Remember, keep celebrating your successes—you're doing great!

Scan the QR code below

CONCLUSION

Now that you've read this book, I hope you're less worried that your relationship with your children will be harmed because you can't manage your anger.

Let me emphasize again what I've repeated throughout the book: nothing is wrong with getting angry—the challenge is to direct your anger. Even when you need to express your anger, you should do so in a way that doesn't harm your relationship with your children and helps resolve the issue that triggered you.

You now know a range of techniques to help you do this. You've learned about the C.A.L.M.S. Anger Management Toolkit. You can identify what makes you angry, especially concerning your children's behavior. You know how to communicate your anger effectively in ways that do not worsen the situation. You know the strategies for maintaining a positive mindset, even in the midst of anger. You understand the importance of support systems since anger, which makes us think we're always right, is difficult to manage without help. You know how to benchmark and track your progress—an essential exercise since what is not measured cannot be understood. And you know the practical strategies for putting all this knowledge into effect.

Keep in mind that the process of managing anger is ongoing. It requires patience, practice, and persistence. The techniques and strategies you've learned are tools to help you navigate challenging situations with your children. Mastery is only achieved through consistent application and a commitment to personal growth.

One of the most critical aspects of anger management is self-awareness. By understanding your triggers and recognizing the early signs of anger, you can take proactive steps to prevent escalation. This self-awareness allows you to pause, reflect, and choose a constructive response rather than reacting impulsively. Remember, it's not about suppressing your anger but about channeling it in a way that is productive and beneficial for both you and your children. Part of this process is understanding different parenting cultures and styles.

Effective communication is another cornerstone of managing anger. It's vital to express your feelings clearly and assertively without being aggressive. When you communicate your anger in a way that is respectful and constructive, you model healthy emotional expression for your children. They learn that it's okay to feel angry, but there are appropriate ways to deal with those feelings.

Maintaining a positive mindset is crucial, especially when dealing with anger. A positive outlook helps you stay calm and composed, even in challenging situations. It allows you to see the bigger picture and not get overwhelmed by momentary frustrations. Techniques such as mindfulness and gratitude can help cultivate this positive mindset. By focusing on the positives in your relationship with your children, you can keep your anger in check and respond more effectively.

Support systems play a significant role in managing anger. Surrounding yourself with people who understand and support your goals can provide much-needed encouragement and accountability. Whether it's a partner, friend, or support group, having someone to talk to can make a big difference. These support systems can offer a fresh perspective and help you stay committed to your anger management journey.

Tracking your progress is an essential part of the process. By keeping a journal or using an app to record your experiences, you can identify patterns and measure your improvement. This tracking helps you stay motivated and focused on your goals. It also provides valuable insights into what works and what needs adjustment. As the British physicist and mathematician William Thomson Kelvin wrote: "What is not defined cannot be measured. What is not measured cannot be improved. What is not improved is always degraded."

Practical strategies are the foundation of effective anger management. Techniques such as deep breathing, time-outs, and physical exercise can help you calm down and regain control. These strategies are not one-size-fits-all, so it's essential to find what works best for you. By experimenting with different techniques and adapting them to your needs, you can develop a personalized anger management plan.

As you continue to apply the C.A.L.M.S. Anger Management Toolkit, remember that setbacks are a natural part of the process. There will be times when you may lose your temper or struggle to manage your anger effectively. It's essential to be kind to yourself and recognize that growth takes time. Each setback is an opportunity to learn and improve.

In addition to the techniques and strategies covered in this book, it's important to seek professional help if needed. Sometimes, anger issues can stem from deeper emotional or psychological problems that require specialized support. A therapist or counselor can provide valuable guidance and help you address underlying issues contributing to your anger.

The journey of managing anger is also about strengthening your relationship with your children. By managing your anger effectively, you create a more positive and supportive environment for your children to thrive. They learn to trust you and feel safe expressing their emotions. This trust fosters a deeper bond and a healthier parent-child relationship.

It's also important to involve your children in the process. Teaching them about anger and how to manage it can empower them with valuable life skills. By setting an example and discussing these concepts openly, you help them develop their emotional intelligence and resilience.

As you reflect on the knowledge and skills you've gained, take a moment to appreciate your progress. Managing anger is not easy, and your commitment to improving yourself and your relationship with your children is commendable. Celebrate your successes, no matter how small, and continue to strive for growth.

Managing anger is a multifaceted and ongoing process. By applying the C.A.L.M.S. Anger Management Toolkit and remaining committed to your personal growth, you can create a healthier and more positive environment for yourself and your children. Keep learning, keep growing, and keep striving for a harmonious and loving family dynamic.

www.ingramcontent.com/pod-product-compliance
Lightning Source LLC
Chambersburg PA
CBHW060935120626
46557CB00003B/1011